Aura

智 **of**

慧

的 **Wisdom**

光

環

by Sheng-yen Lu

Translated by Cheng Yew Chung

Foreword by Professor Shih-I Chu

A US Daden Culture Publication

US Daden Culture LLC
3440 Foothill Blvd.
Oakland, CA 94601
U.S.A.
Website: www.usdaden.com
Email: us.daden.culture@gmail.com

Lu, Sheng-yen, 1945-
The Aura of Wisdom/by Sheng-yen Lu;
translated by Cheng Yew Chung;
edited by Jason Yu;
proofread by Victor Hazen and Janice Gilpin.

Library of Congress Control Number(PCN): 2010929501
ISBN-13: 978-0-9841561-4-6
ISBN-10: 0-9841561-4-3
1. True Buddha School. 2. Chinese-Tantrayana Buddhism.
Cover design and layout by US Daden Culture Design Team
Photograph by US Daden Culture
Set in Minion Pro 12
US Daden books are printed on acid-free paper and meet the guidelines for the permanence and durability set by the Council of Library Resources.

Printed in U.S.A.

ISBN: 978-0-9841561-4-6

9 780984 156146

Special Acknowledgements

The True Buddha Translation Teams (TBTTs) would like to express the highest honor and deepest gratitude to Living Buddha Lian-sheng, Sheng-yen Lu, and Master Lianxiang for their continuing support and guidance on the translation effort. Without their compassion, wisdom, blessings, and encouragement, this project would not have reached fruition.

In addition, we would like to acknowledge the diligent work put forth by the following volunteers on this project: Cheng Yew Chung (translator), Jason Yu (editor), Victor Hazen and Janice Gilpin (proofreaders). We would like to thank these dedicated and selfless volunteers who have contributed their time and effort to promote the works of Living Buddha Lian-sheng, and to support the publications of US Daden Culture.

We would also like to extend our sincere appreciation to all other volunteers who work behind the scenes, facilitating the translation process, and handling administrative responsibilities.

May all volunteers be blessed for their immeasurable merits. May all sentient beings benefit from the ocean of wisdom.

Table of Contents

Table of Contents

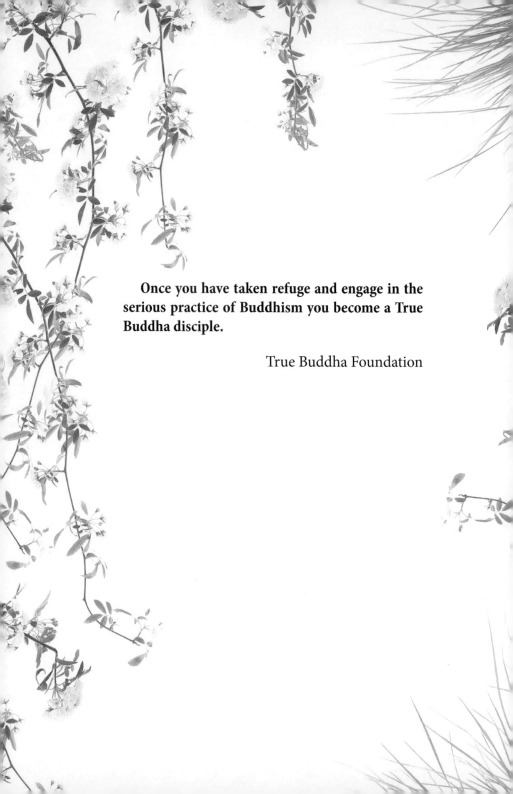

Once you have taken refuge and engage in the serious practice of Buddhism you become a True Buddha disciple.

True Buddha Foundation

Foreword

The Aura of Wisdom - Insights of the Tathagata is the 154th book by the Root Guru of True Buddha School, Living Buddha Lian-sheng. The words of wisdom contained within this book make it extremely precious, for Living Buddha Lian-sheng has managed to encapsulate over thirty years of his actual practice and attainment in ninety short articles. Everything is explained in layman's terms, and presents the fruition of this supreme wisdom as a gift to every Buddhist and reader who has the affinity to receive them. Such is the sincerity and selfless nature of Living Buddha Lian-sheng, whose boundless compassion has guided many practitioners on the right path to practicing Buddhism, providing guidance on the right view of the Buddhadharma, and transmitting the pith instructions and heart essence required to cultivate the extraordinary teachings of Vajrayana.

In the early chapters of this book, Living Buddha Lian-sheng stresses the importance of right view. All Buddhist practitioners must understand and have faith in the teachings of cause, condition and effect, embracing both the practical and theoretical aspects of the Buddhadharma, such as the Three Seals of the Dharma, the Four Noble Truths, the Eightfold Path and the Twelve Links of Dependent Origination. All Vajrayana practitioners must take refuge in a Vajra Master who is a genuine lineage holder, and understand that only through "Honoring the Guru, Treasuring the Dharma and Practicing diligently" will they achieve spiritual attainment. Living Buddha Lian-sheng emphasizes the importance of purifying the mind, as seen in the Vajrayana teachings of transforming the Three Karmas to the Three Secrets, where one attains the purification of body, speech and mind. By cultivating the mind and purifying your thoughts, you shall attain buddhahood. His Holiness also points out that Shakyamuni Buddha transmitted both Sutrayana and Vajrayana teachings as ways of attaining buddhahood. True Buddha School advocates the perfect penetration of the Sutrayana and Vajrayana teachings. Metaphorically speaking, if Sutrayana is seen as a shirt and Vajrayana as the collar, there is no way one can forgo the shirt and wear only the collar.

In chapter twenty-nine, Living Buddha Lian-sheng reveals the secret of Attaining Buddhahood in this Very Body through practicing Vajrayana. The Sutrayana teachings commonly suggest that it would take as long as three Asankhya kalpas to attain buddhahood, which translate into an immeasurable length of time. However, Living Buddha Lian-sheng points out that the reality of three Asankhya kalpas actually describes the countless thoughts that arise from the three poisons of greed, anger and ignorance. If every thought represents one kalpa, it would only mean that once we control and transform the three poisons, we shall transcend the three Asankhya kalpas to attain buddhahood in this lifetime. The Vajrayana teachings hold that you can gain attainment with the three bodies, namely the dharmakaya, the sambhogakaya, and the nirmanakaya, which leads to the attainment of buddhahood in this lifetime. Living Buddha Lian-sheng, in his unsurpassed wisdom, has resolved this theoretical bottleneck with easy to understand explanations, so that all Vajrayana practitioners may receive this truth with joy and generate great bodhicitta.

In one chapter, Heart Essence and Oral Transmissions, Living Buddha Lian-sheng explains the importance of receiving empowerments in the proper order, and how you should also practice and gain spiritual attainment in stages. The Vajrayana practitioner must cultivate the purification of body, speech and mind before embarking on the cultivation of winds, channels and drops. Following that, the practitioner enters the cultivation of the Highest Yoga Tantra, and eventually cultivates the Great Perfection. But with Vajrayana teachings, you must receive their heart essence and oral transmissions directly from a lineage guru. Otherwise, you cannot obtain spiritual achievement.

Living Buddha Lian-sheng also explains the importance of the practice of contemplation and visualization, such as the Merging of Self and Deity Contemplation [called Ruwo-Woru], the Moon Disc Visualization, and the Visualization of the Seed Syllable AH and so forth. His Holiness also points out that the Three Roots of Vajrayana are the Guru, the Personal Deity and the Dharma Protector. The Union of the Three Secrets of Vajrayana refers to the union of the three secrets of body, speech and mind of the practitioner with the corresponding body, speech and mind of his personal deity, touching on the heart essence which explains how they can merge in non-dual oneness. Living Buddha Lian-sheng also emphasizes the importance of the Four Preliminaries and mantras. He transmits many special teachings and their heart essence, such as: the Secret of Contemplating on Emptiness; the Pith Instruction of Entering, Abiding and Absorbing; the Nine Levels of Accomplishment of the True Buddha Tantra; the Importance of Cultivating Qi or Vital Winds; the Protection Method and the Boundary Method; the Jambhala or Wealth Deity Practice; the Art of Knowing the Future; the Secret of Entering Celestial Palaces; the Practice of Harmonization; the Practice of Subjugation; the Way of Receiving Great Wisdom; Oratory Practices; the Stages of Entering into Samadhi; and all the Sadhanas of True Buddha School, among other precious practices.

Living Buddha Lian-sheng, in all compassion and wisdom,

expounds the right view of the Buddhadharma and the very essence of Vajrayana in this book, *The Aura of Wisdom*. Encapsulated in his writings are words of great wisdom, inspiring us as we are guided through the chapters of great insights. In the course of reading it, one senses the outpouring of love and care from His Holiness towards all sentient beings and his disciples. It is as good as receiving the blessing of his wisdom. This book is fundamental to anyone who has just taken refuge in True Buddha School and is starting out in the practice of the True Buddha Tantra. However, for any seasoned Vajrayana practitioner, this book remains a masterpiece that is worth reading again and again. It is my wish that all sentient beings with the right affinity may benefit from this book and receive great wisdom through it. By continuing with the diligent practice of the True Buddha Tantra, the attainment of enlightenment will be within your reach in no time.

Shih-I Chu, Ph.D.
Watkins Distinguished Professor
University of Kansas, U.S.A.
Academician, Academia Sinica, Taiwan

1. Spiritual Conviction

This article is written for disciples who have just taken refuge and have begun their initial practice of the True Buddha Tantra.

Let me say this to you in all honesty. As an enlightened practitioner, I have truly visited the Maha Twin Lotus Ponds and have seen my identity in my past life as Padmakumara himself.

The True Buddha Tantra really is an effective practice that brings tangible results. Besides helping you gain better health and longevity, attracting good fortune and fostering the growth of blessings and wisdom, it also allows you to spontaneously activate the Four Bodies or Kayas, express the Five Wisdoms, manifest the Rainbow Light Body and attain Supreme Bodhi or Enlightenment.

As a novice, it is important that you have faith in the Root Guru, the Buddha, the Dharma, and the Sangha. This is the very heart of your spiritual conviction.

Needless to say, it takes considerable practice in the cultivation of the True Buddha Tantra before you can attain fruition. Do not give up upon meeting slight setbacks. The True Buddha Tantra is aimed at freeing you from your defilements, helping you gain mastery over life and death and become enlightened. To attain these goals, you must remain firm in your spiritual conviction.

In this world, there is one person whose spiritual conviction is always firm, and that person is myself, Living Buddha Lian-sheng, Sheng-yen Lu. I shall never lose my spiritual conviction.

I have faced mountains of disasters in my life. Anyone else in my shoes would have long given up their practice due to these setbacks. The obstacles placed before me have seemed endless, one following after another, and yet my spiritual will has become tempered and sure instead of fading. If I am not a Tathagata, then who is? I have long taken on the role of the Thus Come One.

Let me say this to you: if I have not given up despite all the obstacles I've experienced, how could you give up so easily? Let us put our spiritual conviction to the test and see whose conviction is the strongest!

I want to share this with all True Buddha practitioners, so that we may encourage each other.

Contact Address: Sheng-yen Lu
17102 NE 40th Ct.
Redmond, WA 98052
U.S.A.

2. Arrogance

According to the doctrines of Vajrayana Buddhism, the vajra master [called "lama" in Tibetan Buddhism and "guru" in Sanskrit] embodies the Three Jewels of the Buddha, the Dharma, and the Sangha. He represents Vajrasattva in transmitting the teachings. Hence, the vajra master is very precious and all Vajrayana practitioners must perform a full body prostration before him.

However, with regard to such prostration, some people may feel that the vajra master is promoting the worship of personality, and in so doing, elevating himself above others; this can easily result in the master becoming arrogant. This is the arrogance of being egotistical and looking down on others.

In my view, this is not likely to happen, as I feel that the act of prostration can actually overcome arrogance. My thoughts are:

When a Vajrayana practitioner prostrates before a master, the practitioner's ego is being subdued. And when a master prostrates before his or her root guru, the master's sense of pride is being subdued. Likewise, when the root guru prostrates before the lineage gurus, the root guru's ego is being subdued.

Hence the sequence in True Buddha School: the Vajrayana practitioner prostrates before the master, the master prostrates before myself, and I in turn prostrate before my master, [such as] Vajra Master Thubten Dargye.

I may be Living Buddha Lian-sheng, Sheng-yen Lu, the manifestation of Padmakumara, who is a manifestation of Amitabha Buddha. Nonetheless, it matters little what sort of divine manifestation you are, for you must still prostrate before your guru when you meet him. Thus, regardless of how great your spiritual attainment is, you must kneel and prostrate before your vajra master. The practitioner must first subdue his or her own ego.

Shakyamuni Buddha once said, "If ego is not removed, then even if you have some achievement in meditation, you shall certainly become an Asura King or a Mara King."

True Buddha practitioners, please keep this in mind: if you overcome your ego, you are a buddha; if you remain proud and egotistical, you are a mara.

3. Adopting a Monastic Life

For those who are committed to cultivation, I encourage you to be ordained as monks or nuns. The meaning of adopting a monastic life is so that you can better concentrate on your cultivation, focusing solely on spreading the Dharma. In principle, choosing a monastic life is an act of offering your body and mind to Shakyamuni Buddha. Therefore this pure act of celibacy is worthy of our praise.

However, not everyone has the affinity to take up a monastic life. Thus, it is not mandatory that you lead a monastic life. A practitioner can cultivate as a lay Buddhist, as everything should be done naturally. Hence, it is equally good whether you adopt a monastic life or not.

In True Buddha School, you must consider these three factors when deciding whether to lead a monastic life:

1. Do you suffer from any handicaps or chronic illnesses? Do you have any mental illnesses? Do you have a bad record of criminal offenses?
2. Do you have consent from your parents or spouse?
3. Can you undertake the loneliness and simple lifestyle de-

manded of a life of cultivation?

I feel that these three points are of utmost importance. When you have thought through these issues clearly, then you can take up a monastic life.

If after a while you feel that the monastic lifestyle does not suit your preferences, you can always choose to return to secular life. You are free to choose, and no one can stop you from returning to secular life. Once you grow your hair, remove your monk's robe or lama outfit, you have returned to secular life. Returning to secular life is nothing to be ashamed of, as you can still continue with your practice of the True Buddha Tantra. The only difference is that you have chosen not to practice full time.

Thus, I feel that to lead a monastic life is a bold move, but those lay Buddhists who have attained enlightenment at home are even more remarkable for their achievements.

All my life I have upheld the ideals of freedom and democracy. It would be a crime to impose anything on anyone under the banner of True Buddha School.

4. Manifestations

I once approached the Golden Mother of the Jade Pond with this question, "What is a manifestation?"

The Golden Mother replied, "Straw-headed deities." What this term means is that manifestations are as numerous as the blades of grass that spread over the vast earth. Thus, the celestial deities have given a nickname to these manifestations: "straw-headed deities."

For example:

"Homage to the 36 trillion, 119 thousand and 500 Amitabha Buddhas."

"The trillions of manifestations of Vairocana Buddha."

"Buddha Locana manifested in six hundred thousand kotis of nayutas of yojanas, multiplied by the number of the grains of sand of the Ganges River."

Even Avalokitesvara Bodhisattva manifests thirty-two forms, and each manifested form in turn manifests infinite bodies. Thus such manifestations are infinite in number. These manifestations are part of the natural order of the universe, and also are due to the power of transformation.

To my knowledge, the manifestations of Padmakumara are countless in number. Among the disciples of True Buddha School are many manifestations of Padmakumara. I am only one of them, and you can say I have achieved enlightenment a bit earlier. Thus, I am the enlightened straw-headed deity of White Padmakumara.

I have identified many manifestations of the Golden Mother of the Jade Pond, including Master Lianci, Senior Reverend Lianhua Chunlian, Lianhua Youzhen, Lianhua Suming, and so on.

I personally feel that the manifestations of all deities are indeed respectable. However, these manifestations cover the land like grass, just like the moon mirrors itself in water. The buddha pure lands are manifestations, and the manifestations of deities are no different.

When you know you are a manifestation, it is even more important that you tread carefully and follow the right Dharma, have the right understanding, uphold the right view and maintain right mindfulness. You should cultivate properly and propagate the Dharma with your heart. You must recognize the truth that a manifestation is only an illusory body like a bubble, and if you are trapped in material defilement, you shall be drawn into the six realms of transmigration!

Straw-headed deity! If you are tainted and fall from grace, once burned, you shall be forever lost without leaving a trace behind!

5. Spiritual Response

It is relatively easy to receive spiritual responses through the cultivation of Vajrayana teachings. This is a well known fact. It is due largely to the vajra master, who embodies the Three Jewels of the Buddha, the Dharma, and the Sangha. He holds the immeasurable merits of all the buddhas, and has the remarkable power of blessings.

An enlightened vajra master may bless a person who keeps a firm and pure faith but has yet to begin any form of practice. This is like a person holding a jug of Dharma milk and pouring it into the empty bowl of the receiver. The person who is blessed immediately receives the Dharma milk which fills his or her being, achieving the fulfillment of spiritual response.

In Vajrayana, it is common to have a person who has not done any prior cultivation, and who has just taken refuge or received empowerment, and yet is able to gain immediate response.

If you experience a string of responses and spiritual phenomena, it is important to remain calm, and treat these events as normal occurrences. Your mind should maintain a sense of balance, and ideally remain in a state of non-attachment and renunciation. Whether you have spiritual responses or not is perfectly fine, for we should not be too attached to such matters.

When you have responses, you may talk to a master, or relate them to your fellow disciples. It is best to share your experiences with a master, and use your responses as a basis of encouragement among disciples. Refrain from telling outsiders. Why? People outside your spiritual circle may not believe in such matters, and you may invite criticism, causing more afflictions instead.

A person with spiritual responses should be cautioned against showing off his or her experiences, which would be a display of pride. Know that ego is the seed of the mara, and many have fallen into the path of mara upon receiving spiritual responses due to this mentality. Hence, the further you cultivate with such a mindset, the further you deviate from the righ View, completely unaware of being on the wrong path.

If your body, speech and mind are pure, it is normal to receive responses.

If you persist in cultivation, it is also normal to receive responses from the respective deities and dharma protectors.

You must not think that you have attained the highest spiritual state, and surpassed the achievements of all dharma friends, monks, nuns, and masters. When such a thought arises, you are being deluded by mara.

6. Purification of the Mind

A disciple once approached me with an offering and said, "Guru, please teach me how to gain great spiritual powers."

I replied, "What I teach is how to purify the mind, not how to gain spiritual powers."

My disciple asked, "Isn't it true that buddhas have spiritual powers?"

I said, "Buddhas do have spiritual powers, but those with spiritual powers are not necessarily buddhas."

I told him that even ghosts have powers, and so do good and evil beings. The mara has spiritual powers, and so do non-Buddhist followers. Spiritual powers are an incidental phenomena, a by-product of your cultivation in Buddhism. People should not be attached to such phenomenal powers, or they will risk going astray onto the wrong path.

If you focus on cultivating spiritual powers, it will be easy to cling to those states. Wild and meandering thoughts will arise, leading you into delusion.

Eventually you shall fall into the grasp of mara. When you are attracted to various spiritual powers, you will deviate from the Buddha's teachings and turn yourself into a demon of some kind.

What exactly does the Buddha teach us? It is still this familiar saying:

Not to do any evil, to carry out all good deeds, to purify the mind: this is the teaching of the buddhas.

I have written over a hundred fifty books. Seriously speaking, I can summarize the millions of words I've written into four words:

"Purification of the Mind."

In Vajrayana Buddhism, the three karmas are transformed into three secrets: the secret of the body, the secret of speech, and the secret of the mind. The purification of the body, speech and mind is essentially the "purification of the mind!"

The act of cultivating your heart and purifying your mind leads you to buddhahood. To only develop spiritual powers leads you to becoming a mara. If you are a practicing True Buddha Tantra cultivator, you need to discern these matters carefully!

7. Right View

Right view is listed first in the Eightfold Path, indicating its importance. Right view means having the correct perspective - it
refers to a Buddhist having faith, acceptance and understanding about
the truth of cause and effect, the practice and doctrines of Buddhism,
the Three Seals of the Dharma, the Four Noble Truths, the Eightfold
Path, and the Twelve Links of Dependent Origination.

The right view of Vajrayana teachings is vital. It is essential that a
Vajrayana practitioner takes refuge in a vajra master who is a true lineage holder. This means that it is necessary to identify and ascertain
a root guru whom you are willing to follow and trust completely, so
that you may focus wholeheartedly on your cultivation. It is only by
placing your attention on the root guru and often contemplating his
image will you have the possibility of reaching a state of immovable
calm. This is the right view of Vajrayana Buddhism.

The present mix of Buddhist teachings in the world does not necessarily reflect the true doctrine of Buddhism. A multitude of denominations have sprung up to actively promote themselves and attract a
following, either by highlighting their respective skills, their ability to

communicate with spirits, the use of qigong, or even by resorting to the means of using ghosts to deceive men and women.

These sects attract a following for the purpose of conning people out of their donations and offerings, and expanding their territories through entirely unscrupulous means. Many who lack the right view have fallen into these wrong paths and cannot extricate themselves from the influences of these paths. They feel they have found an enlightened master from whom they can study the supreme teachings, and feel they are nearing buddhahood. Actually they have long fallen prey to mara.

These individuals should reflect on the right view of Vajrayana Buddhism as having one root guru, one personal deity, and one dharma protector, and practice accordingly. Do not covet spiritual powers and evil sorcery. Do not covet special arts or learning numerous practices. Avoid attachment to illusory visions and sounds. Do not believe slander and do not become doubtful.

Do not believe anything blindly, and turn away from superstition. It is important to use common sense.

Ask yourself, do you or do you not hold the right view? To achieve attainment in Vajrayana and gain liberation from samsara, you must maintain the right view all the way through!

8. A True Acharya

During the time when I was transmitting the Kalachakra Practice, Vajra Master Thubten Dargye personally penned this authorization: "The Kalachakra lineage shall hereby be transmitted to Thubten Qimo. This constitutes the Samaya Pledge." This transmission of Dharma is thus the lineage itself, and a true acharya or vajra master will definitely must have a lineage. [Note: Thubten Qimo is Living Buddha Lian-sheng's Gelugpa Dharma name.]

I have the Dharma hat of Milarepa, the Dharma robe of Ganden Tripa, the Dharma seal belonging to a Sakya throne holder, a vajra, a vajra bell and a bottle belonging to lineage gurus, practice texts transmitted personally by lineage gurus, and so on. These are the authenticating objects given only to a true vajra master.

Among the precious authenticating objects are two which I am most proud of: a clay statue of Vajrapani Bodhisattva and a clay statue of Vajravarahi molded personally by Kanjurwa Khutughtu himself. These two treasures are presently kept at the Rainbow Villa. They have been passed down from Kanjurwa Khutughtu to Vajra Master Thubten Dargye, who in turn handed them to me.

Entrusted with the lineage transmission of Vajrayana practices, I "honor the guru, treasure the dharma, and practice diligently," which has lead to spiritual attainment. At this time I have even greater compassion for sentient beings and have aspired great bodhicitta. I vow to spread the teachings and practices of Buddhism to the world and take on the responsibilities of the Tathagata, devoting my life to the Buddha.

I have a firm belief in my lineage. I have absolute faith in the True Buddha Tantra. I have attained spiritual resonance [spiritual response or union] with all teachings, and I have attracted the presence of a hundred thousand dakinis to applaud and celebrate my attainment.

My personal deity appeared and said to me, "Do not own any temple. Do not hold on to any territory. Do not keep any personal wealth. If you gain the world, you shall lose heaven. You, Living Buddha Liansheng, have attained perfect spirituality. You have great compassion and have developed and attained the Five Wisdoms. Your virtue is pure and noble, and you have overcome all life and death. You have risen above all delusions."

If someone were to ask me what constitutes a true acharya or vajra master, my reply would be, "Please go through this chapter carefully!"

9. Self Importance

Master Ching Hai once told her disciples, "Presently, there are indeed some enlightened masters in this world. I am an enlightened master. When you find me, there is no further need to search for others, for I am the one."

What Master Ching Hai said is fair and modest enough.

Someone by the name of Li who started a certain "Gong" movement once said, "The Dharma transmitted by Shakyamuni Buddha is just a minor teaching. The Dharma or Fa that I transmit is Dafa, or major teaching. In the past, man cultivated Dharma. Today it is Dharma or Fa that cultivates man."

Someone asked Mr. Li, "Presently, who is liberating sentient beings in this world?"

Mr. Li said, "Only me. There is no other."

What this statement implies is that Mr. Li feels that he is the only "Buddha" in the whole world, whereas other people are merely maras. He once commented that a senior monk was a manifestation of maras, and that Sri Sathya Sai Baba was possessed by a serpent spirit. The Japanese Aum Shinrikyo cult was derived from ghosts of hell.

The qigong masters from mainland China are all being possessed by animal spirits.

Mr. Li says his path is the only right path.

I also know of a certain Mr. Xiao who claims, "I am the manifestation of Vairocana, the Lord of tens of thousands of buddhas in the universe. Sheng-yen Lu is only a tiny little buddha who is under my jurisdiction."

All right! The reason I wrote this article is to convey the message that everyone may have claimed to have attained realization and reached enlightenment, saying others are all bad and that he or she alone is the greatest, praising themselves and discrediting others, competing to beat others in the game of being the biggest and highest in spiritual attainment.

I just want to say this to you, that as someone who is studying and practicing Buddhism, you need to open your eyes to discern:

Who is really being egotistical?

Who is really praising himself or herself and discrediting others?

Who really has wonderful teachings?

Who is able to remain undistracted?

Who is the perfectly enlightened hermit?

10. The Four Levels of Empowerments

True Buddha School offers many empowerments. The meaning of empowerment is: "The vajra master, representing all deities, empowers his disciples with a pure Dharma transmission."

The four levels of empowerments cover empowerments ranging from simple to advanced levels, moving from the initial stage of practice to the Great Perfection, which is the highest of all empowerments.

The first level of empowerment - the purification of body, speech and mind.

The second level of empowerment - the practice of vital winds, channels and drops.

The third level of empowerment - the Highest Yoga Tantra.

The fourth level of empowerment - the Great Perfection.

In general, disciples of True Buddha School who have received the first level of empowerment are the most numerous. The empowerments they have received include the empowerment of many deities, the empowerment of the Four Preliminary Practices, the empowerment of Guru Yoga, and so on.

Disciples who have received the second level of empowerment

are lesser in number. This empowerment includes the practice of inner fire, the practice of drops, and the method of non-leakage. The non-leakage method is only transmitted to selected students who are proper "dharma vessels."

The third level of empowerment, the Highest Yoga Tantra, has been given only to one individual so far. Only a certain vajra master has received it. The fourth level of empowerment the Great Perfection has not been given to anyone yet.

I must state that as long as you keep your body, speech and mind pure, you are certain to gain rebirth in a Buddha pure land. The achievement of practicing vital winds, channels and drops leads to the attainment of the Indestructible Vajra Body. The achievement of practicing the Highest Yoga Tantra is the attainment of the Pure Light of Bliss. To achieve the Great Perfection is to enter into Emptiness and become enlightened in this present lifetime, attaining the Rainbow Accomplishment.

Why is it that the second, third and fourth levels of empowerment are granted to a much smaller number of disciples?

I have said that the first level of empowerment leads to the purity of body, speech and mind. This purity is the cleansing of the poisons of greed, anger and ignorance. If you think about it, the cleansing of greed, anger and ignorance is already very difficult for people of this modern age.

I (Living Buddha Lian-sheng, Sheng-yen Lu) possess the most precious Dharma treasures which are priceless and beyond comparison.

Let me say this, "If you have courage and great aspirations for enlightenment, then come along!"

11. Making Offerings

In the old days of Tibetan Buddhism, when a disciple received an empowerment, he would be required to make an offering of several cows and sheep to his lama. The greater the teaching, the larger the number of cows and sheep required for the offering.

Most interesting was the case of Lama Ngokpa when he approached Marpa to request the empowerment of a practice which belonged to the Highest Yoga Tantra class. Marpa said, "You must be detached from all attachments and obstacles, for this empowerment requires that you offer all your wealth to the guru."

Lama Ngokpa did not hesitate and drove all his cows and sheep to Marpa's place and offered them to him - all except for a sheep with a bad leg which he felt Marpa would likely reject. Marpa was aware of it, and told the lama, "All wealth means everything, including the lame sheep." Thus, Lama Ngokpa returned with the sheep with a bad limb and offered it to Marpa.

According to the doctrines of Vajrayana Buddhism, the teachings of the Highest Yoga Tantra are very precious. In order to make the disciples appreciate and treasure such teachings, a precious offering is required.

It is said that gold, silver and precious jewels represent an attachment and a great obstacle that all cultivators face. Hence, it is important that you learn to give and offer them.

Yet with me, it is "offer as you wish!" Please do not think that my Vajrayana teachings are any less precious or rare, or that they are anything but the most precious and supreme teachings.

I have my reasons for doing this. The teachings of the Highest Yoga Tantra which I have received cannot be had for any amount of money, jewels, diamonds, cars or houses.

I only ask that you offer to keep your body, speech and mind cleansed everyday, and to take your practice seriously. When everyone is able to reach attainment sooner and proceed to propagate the Dharma and liberate sentient beings, enlightening oneself and others along the way, such an offering of Dharma would be the greatest offering to me.

12. Making Offerings (2)

The significance of making offerings to higher beings are: bringing us closer to them, service, and respect. Offerings also apply
to giving to those who are less fortunate, signifying sympathy, compassion, and care.

When practicing the Six Perfections of Generosity, Discipline, Patience, Effort, Meditation and Wisdom, it is Generosity that ranks
first.

Generosity is divided into the generosity of giving wealth, the generosity of giving Dharma, and the generosity of giving fearlessly.

I like to quote a passage from the *Diamond Sutra*: "Moreover, Subhuti, if a man or woman brought together as many piles of the seven
jewels as all the Mount Sumerus in the billion worlds of the Universe
and gave them as offerings, and a noble son or daughter grasped but
a single four line gatha of this Dharma teaching of the Perfection
of Wisdom and made it known to others, Subhuti, the noble son or
daughter's body of merit would be greater by more than a hundred-
fold, indeed, by an amount beyond comparison."

This illustrates that of all offerings, the offering of Dharma ranks supreme.

The generosity of wealth offers aid to physical, mundane existence, whereas the generosity of Dharma offers liberation to your spiritual existence. The generosity of wealth is temporary, but the generosity of Dharma promises true liberation from suffering, allowing sentient beings to attain happiness, to leave the wheel of samsara, and to be free from life and death. Thus, the generosity of Dharma is enduring.

I observe that today's Buddhist schools are practicing just the opposite, in which the generosity of wealth ranks the first, and there is nothing on the giving of Dharma. It is pathetic indeed!

These Buddhist schools are building majestic temples, hospitals, universities, television stations, attracting many people to give money, but there is very little in the giving of Dharma. It is certainly a sorry state.

Let me emphasize this:

The followers of True Buddha School need not make offerings to me, their root guru, with money and jewels. When you practice the True Buddha Tantra sincerely, you are making offerings to me.

I hold limitless treasures, for I am the Great Blessing Vajra. These treasures are not of this earth, but of the heavens.

13. Spiritual Validation

A person who just took refuge in Vajrayana Buddhism decided to put on a Pandita hat and a Dharma robe, and took a photo of himself. He sent the photo to me and asked that I confer on him the title of the XX throne holder.

I asked him, "Why did you do this?"

He replied, "I have been unemployed for some time and decided that I could make a career of being a throne holder."

I asked, "What are the Four Classes of Tantra of Vajrayana Buddhism?" He could not answer. So I then said, "The Four Classes of Tantra, being Kriya Tantra [Action], Charya Tantra [Performance], Yoga Tantra and Anuttarayoga Tantra [Highest Yoga Tantra], require validation at each stage of accomplishment. Have you received validation?"

He appeared lost, and asked me what exactly validation was.

Let me state this clearly to all of you. In practicing the sadhanas of Vajrayana Buddhism, you must cultivate them in incremental stages:

1. You need to seek out a vajra master who is truly a lineage

holder, take refuge in him, and receive empowerment.

2.   You must have pure faith in the transmission of your guru's teachings, and learn their secrets.

3.   You must practice sincerely.

4.   You must cultivate and attain spiritual resonance with the
respective stages. Seek validation and guidance from your
vajra master. If the validation is true, then move to the
next higher level, cultivate in stages, and receive validation in stages.

The person mentioned in this short chapter was being preposter-
ous, believing that he would become a master, thus deceiving himself
and others into believing that he would become a throne holder. If
you are not being honest in your cultivation and covet fame and fortune, doesn't it seem absurd and laughable?

When the actual practice of each sadhana in Vajrayana Buddhism
reveals its corresponding spiritual experience, it must be validated by
a master. One may mistake the false for the real, and regard illusion as
reality. If the disciple does not believe in the instruction of his guru,
he is vulnerable to being trapped in the mara realms, without self-
awareness.

You can't simply buy a Pandita hat and a Dharma robe and start
wearing them!

They are to be given to you after validation by your root guru!

14. Keeping the Codes and Precepts

Some assume that Vajrayana Buddhism is rather lax and disregards the keeping of codes and precepts. Let me correct this by saying that this is a major misconception of the Vajrayana teachings and is an inaccurate view!

Any Buddhist, regardless of his affinity with Sutrayana or Vajrayana Buddhism, knows the necessity of keeping discipline. It is necessary to learn the Three Principles of Discipline, Meditation, and Wisdom.

"Discipline" refers to the ending of all evil actions.

"Meditation" refers to the stability of mind in one pointedness.

"Wisdom" refers to the breaking of illusion to experience reality.

What this means is, simply through discipline, the pure mind finds peace, and when the mind finds peace, it is easier to enter into deep meditation. With deep meditation, it is possible to perceive all things clearly, allowing wisdom to arise.

There are many sets of precepts and codes in Buddhism, including the Five Precepts, the Eight Precepts, the Ten Precepts, the Bodhisattva Vows, the Two Hundred and Fifty Monastic Rules, and so on. Both Sutrayana and Vajrayana Buddhism must observe these precepts and codes.

In Vajrayana Buddhism, they include the Fifty Stanzas on Guru Devotion, the Fourteen Root Vows of Vajrayana, Silavrata Paramarsa [the mistaken view of adherence to ascetic practices in the belief that they will bring release], Pratimoksa [vows of personal liberation], natural moral laws, and so on. From what I know, the codes of Vajrayana Buddhism are more detailed and precise than the Mahayana and Hinayana codes.

When a Vajrayana code is breached, it results in you entering the Vajra Hell. Its severe karmic consequences include:

Swallowing burning hot iron pellets, drinking hot molten iron, wearing hot metallic shirts, and sitting on burning hot iron beds. No release date is ever set for one who occupies Vajra Hell, which is dreadful indeed.

One must strictly observe the precepts and codes when cultivating the True Buddha Tantra. When Shakyamuni Buddha entered Nirvana, he wanted his disciples to abide by the precepts as their guide, for discipline is the very foundation of accomplishment.

If anyone were to suggest that you can attain buddhahood without having to abide by the precepts, it would be a breach of the Samaya Pledge.

Let me say this, "If there were no upholding of the precepts, how could humans and heavenly beings ever have faith? If you do not keep precepts, it is against the way of the wise, and you shall find yourself among the foolish. There can be no liberation from life and death, and no ending of the wandering in samsara!"

15. The Spirit of Upholding the Precepts

Since ancient times, the spirit of keeping precepts has been empha-
sized so that people see the importance of observing precepts and the
Buddhadharma can be preserved on earth.

When receiving the precepts, the master would ask his disciple,
"Can you tolerate the Ten Acts?"

The disciple replied, "Yes, I can."

What are these Ten Acts? They are, in fact, rather appalling:

1. Cutting your flesh to feed eagles.
2. Giving up your body to feed a tiger.
3. Cutting off your head to thank the heavens.
4. Breaking your bones to extract the marrow.
5. Cutting parts of your body to light a lamp.
6. Digging out your eyes to give them to someone.
7. Slicing your skin to provide material on which to write the
   sutras.
8. Piercing your heart to ascertain the extent of your deter-
   mination.

9. Setting your body in flames to offer to the Buddha.
10. Piercing your body so that your blood may be sprinkled on the floor.

These Ten Acts are depicted in the Mahayana Bodhisattva Vows to illustrate the spirit of self-sacrifice. Of course, I am not asking you to do these things, for these are self-abusive acts which I feel are inappropriate for our times. Yet, if you have taken the oath, and can tolerate the Ten Acts, then you cannot break vows when it is convenient. I mean, you would at least have learned the spirit of ancient practitioners who could uphold precepts in the strictest manner!

Today, many in True Buddha School have taken the Bodhisattva Vows, and a number of disciples follow the Monastic Codes as well. Yet few could truly uphold and sustain the discipline of keeping precepts. This is something that disappoints me. I could not detect the slightest spirit of discipline in them, and this is really discouraging!

I say this to you in all honesty:

One who is well versed with the precepts and strictly abides in them is known as a Vinaya Master.

One who practices Zen meditation and attains self realization is known as a Zen Master.

One who is clear about both Sutrayana and Vajrayana doctrines, and cultivates and propagates them, is known as a Dharma Master.

When you combine all three roles in one, you become a true vajra master.

16 True Buddha School

People who criticize True Buddha School love to say, "So you consider yourself the True Buddha? Doesn't that make us false buddhas?"

When I heard this, I found it rather laughable. My view is this, "I have been to the Dharma Nature (or Dharmakaya) Land where the Dharmakaya (Truth Body) of the Buddha resides, and have validated the existence of the Dharmakaya and the Sambhogakaya (Bliss Body) of the Buddha. I am completely aware of the existence of the True Buddha Siddhi. Therefore, I decided to establish my own school and name it True Buddha School."

I want to emphasize this: when Shakyamuni Buddha appeared on earth, he reached out to those who had affinity with him, studied the capacities and intelligence of sentient beings, and offered them the appropriate antidotes according to their spiritual conditions. When the Buddha entered Nirvana, his disciples formed different schools in response to his teachings, and collectively assembled the Buddhist Canon [the Tripitaka]. In reality, all aspects of the Dharma are inter-linked, and when they are interpenetrated, they express the Dharma wonderfully. Hence, all schools in essence express the True Buddha.

I mean to say that I am the True Buddha, and so are you. As long as it is the Buddhadharma, it is the True Buddha. I would not criticize others as being false buddhas.

If one takes to the study of Prajna and its corresponding sutras, one may follow Zen Buddhism.

If one takes to the study of the *Amitabha Sutra*, the *Larger Sutra* on Amitayus, or the *Sutra on Contemplation of Amitayus*, one may follow Pure Land Buddhism.

If one takes to the study of the *Mahavairocana Sutra* and the *Vajrasekhara Sutra*, one may follow Vajrayana Buddhism.

If one takes to the study of the *Brahmajala Sutra*, one may follow the Vinaya tradition of Buddhism.

If one takes to the study of the *Madhyamaka Sastra* (the *Treatise of the Middle Way*), *Sata Sastra* (*The One Hundred Verse Treatise*), or the *Dvadasanikaya Sastra* (the *Twelve Gate Treatise*), one may follow the Three Sastras School of Buddhism [also known as Sanlun, a Chinese Madhyamaka School].

If one takes to the study of the three primary texts of the *Lotus Sutra*, one may follow the Tiantai School of Buddhism.

If one takes to the study of the *Avatamsaka Sutra* [or the *Flower Garland Sutra*], one may follow the Huayan or Avatamsaka School of Buddhism.

If one takes to the study of the *Lankavatara Sutra*, the *Samdhinirmocana Sutra*, the *Vijnaptimatratasiddhi Sastra* and the *Yogacarabhumi Sastra*, one may follow the Consciousness-Only or Dharmalaksana School of Buddhism.

Due to my deeper affinity with Vajrayana Buddhism, I have selected the very best of its teachings from my studies of it, and have established the best raft to ferry sentient beings across the ocean of samsara and place them on the shore of nirvana.

I have truly validated the existence of the Dharmakaya (Truth

Body) and the Sambhogakaya (Bliss Body) of the Buddha, and validated the presence of the Realm of the True Buddha Siddhi. Thus, True Buddha School is able to deliver sentient beings of affinity based on these causes and circumstances!

This True Buddha School which I have established thus harmonizes with all the schools. The True Buddha exists where Buddhadharma is taught, and there is no reason for mutual rejection. I am true, so is everyone. For those who have a natural inclination toward deep contemplation, please think it over carefully!

Practice with perseverance and patience. Never yearn for mystical powers and never look for short cuts. Be practical and sincere with your cultivation!

Sheng-yen Lu

17. True Practice

I remember one night when I was performing my duties for Taichung's South Gate Bridge land surveying unit, an invisible spiritual teacher descended and then taught me Vajrayana over a period of
three years, averaging an hour per night.

Back then, my arms and legs were often manipulated by the invisible spiritual master, and these experiences made me realize that gods
and spirits really do exist in this universe; that there is such a thing as
a "spiritual world," and the "invisible" does exist. I hence made a vow
that this shall be my conviction in life and I would cultivate earnestly.

Once I was lazy and uttered, "Why should I bother to learn this?
In times of need, all it takes is the help of my invisible teacher to settle
things for me."

I was reprimanded for making such a statement!

I have studied the Vajrayana teachings for many years, entering
into retreat for three years at the Ling Xian (Spiritual Immortal) Villa
in Seattle, USA. It has been thirty years since the Golden Mother of
the Jade Pond initiated the opening of my divine eye. I feel that my
only strong point is my persistence in cultivation, sincerely practicing

daily without fail.

My blood type is "O," depicting a strong character with great patience. When faced with any assignment, I will complete it, no matter what. I am down-to-earth, and shun laziness. You can say I am silly and idiotic, but I am very serious and committed to my cultivation.

I often say that writing and practice are the two important duties of my life, and they are activities I must perform daily. My writing improves over time, as does my spiritual practice. No one can ever take that away from me!

Let me say this to you. I am a true vajra master. On what basis do I say this? I say this on the basis that I diligently practice the True Buddha Tantra daily, without fail.

There are many pseudo-masters among us in today's society, and they all claim, "With a single empowerment, the three main channels shall circulate freely."

"With a single empowerment, the sacred embryo shall be formed."

"With a single empowerment, one shall live to be more than a hundred years old."

"With a single empowerment, the Dharma Wheel shall spin on its own, and one will not need to make any effort in cultivation."

How true are such claims? Please do not ask me. You may refer to the words of Padmasambhava, who said, "honor the guru, treasure the dharma, and practice diligently."

Please remember this:

Practice with perseverance and patience. Never yearn for mystical powers and never look for short cuts. Be practical and sincere with your cultivation!

18. Respecting the Guru

When I first studied Buddhism, I learned from many masters. I took refuge in Venerable Yinshun, Venerable Leguo, Venerable Daoan, Reverend Liaoming, Vajra Master Thubten Dargye, His Holiness the Sixteenth Gyalwa Karmapa, Vajra Master Sakya Zhengkong, Vajra Master Pufang and others.

I received my Bodhisattva Vows from the Masters of Precepts, Venerable Xiandun, Venerable Huisan, and Venerable Jueguang. I learned the recitation of sutra and the repentance ritual from Venerable Shanci and Venerable Shanglin.

My invisible spiritual teachers are the Eminent Sanshan-Jiuhou and Padmasambhava.

I am always prepared to serve my teachers, and I believe completely in the teachings they transmit. I shall always remember what they taught me and shall abide by their instructions without fail.

Of course my teachers lectured me, but I never once talked back to them. I exercised tolerance, as I felt my teachers were giving me lessons on the Perfection of Patience. I have always been respectful to my teachers.

I once took refuge in a vajra master (whose name is not listed here). His teachings and behavior had violated the Buddhist precepts and Buddhadharma. My affinity with him was thus inadequate, and I decided to stay away from him. Still, I maintain my respect for him, and I will not criticize him, simply because he had once taught me.

What I mean is that I am respectful to any teacher who has taught me at one time or another, and I shall always abide by their instructions.

When Padmasambhava rode on his horse and ascended to the sky, he said, "Only those who honor the guru, treasure the dharma and practice diligently shall attain enlightenment."

I have indeed lived up to this statement. I am aware that without the empowerment of a vajra master with lineage, it is absolutely impossible to gain accomplishment in Vajrayana cultivation.

Let me share this with you, "All accomplished Vajrayana adepts are respectful to their masters, and have attained spiritual resonance with them."

Only a fool would believe that a person who is disrespectful to his guru is able to attain great accomplishment.

19. The Most Comprehensive System of Buddhist Practice

Many students of Buddhism like to go "dharma shopping." They try out different schools of Buddhism and wander from one school of thought to the next. Sentient beings are fickle, and fluid like water. One moment, they will flow to the east, and then the next moment you will find them in the west.

I once heard this rumor: "Living Buddha Lian-sheng, Sheng-yen Lu himself has taken refuge with several dozen gurus and ordained monks. If I aspire to be like him, taking refuge and receiving empowerments from teachers everywhere, what is wrong with that?"

When the person advising against such behavior heard this argument, he felt it made sense, and could not refute it.

Today, I am offering my response to that. Anyone who wishes to study the Buddhadharma may explore other Buddhist schools of thought, not so much for thrills, but so that they may draw comparisons between the respective teachings. After you gain a clear picture of the teachings of True Buddha School, and you are satisfied with what they can offer, it isn't too late to take refuge in me.

I do not stop people from seeking out and visiting virtuous teachers. On the other hand, you may want to take a look at what the True Buddha Tantra has to offer. From the Four Preliminary Practices to the Great Perfection, external to internal practices, worldly to transcendental practices, Deity Yoga to Heruka Practices, common to uncommon practices, fire and water offerings, and even the supreme teachings of Tibetan Buddhism - such as Dzogchen, Mahamudra, Lamdre, and the Yamantaka practice - all are included in the system of the True Buddha Tantra.

The True Buddha Tantra is the most comprehensive system of Buddhist practice. Whatever you want to learn and study is offered here.

I can honestly tell everyone that whatever practices you wish to learn from other schools, I have included them in True Buddha School, presented in their most authentic and reliable form. You will even find practices unavailable elsewhere. I am an accomplished adept who epitomizes the teachings and practices of all Buddhist schools.

When you take refuge in Living Buddha Lian-sheng, Sheng-yen Lu, it is equivalent to taking refuge in dozens of gurus and ordained teachers. Is that not sufficient?

In fact, it should be said that when one takes refuge in True Buddha School, one has reached the definitive teaching. One will not find any other school with as comprehensive a system as ours. If one still wishes to run around aimlessly from one school to another like a headless chicken, one deserves to be spanked!

20. Do Not Slander the Vajrayana Teachings

When I first started studying Buddhism, many articles were written to smear the Vajrayana teachings. I came across some of these articles, and found that most of the criticisms were aimed at the practices of devas [or gods]. Their inclusion into mainstream Buddhist doctrines was said to have mixed Brahmanism with Buddhism. The articles went so far as to suggest that Vajrayana Buddhism is Brahmanism.

Some articles suggested that the cultivation of vital winds, channels and drops was not expounded by the Buddha himself, but rather derived from the heretical practice of subtle energies or qigong, which aspires to clear and circulate the Triple Warmer, generate the Macrocosmic and Microcosmic Circulations, and cultivate the generative (jing), vital (qi) and spirit (shen) energies [note: these are terms from Taoism and traditional Chinese medicine]. Thus, on this basis they claimed that the practice of vital winds, channels, and drops were not Buddhist teachings.

There was criticism directed at the practice of Tantra Yoga taught in Vajrayana Buddhism. They felt it had derived from one of the denominations of Hinduism, and should be regarded as a heretical sect with deviant practices. Such criticisms were numerous, and among these articles, some were directed at the practice of homa (fire offering) in Vajrayana Buddhism, noting its similarity with Zoroastrianism, which originated in Persia.

I am aware that Venerable Hongyi once mentioned in a speech that he had criticized Vajrayana Buddhism in the past, and had felt that its teachings were heresy and misleading. Subsequently, having read the Commentary on the *Mahavairocana Sutra*, he gained a better insight into the Vajrayana teachings, and realized that Vajrayana Buddhism embodies layers of deeper meanings. He has since repented.

Venerable Hongyi felt that one should not dwell on the surface of Vajrayana teachings, but go deeper into their inner doctrines. Once they are understood, one would not criticize the Vajrayana teachings anymore.

The act of slandering Vajrayana Buddhism is a grave offense of slandering the Dharma. When people go about slandering Vajrayana Buddhism without thinking, avoid joining in their attacks.

Due to the profound doctrines expounded by the Vajrayana or Esoteric School, its practices were not readily revealed to the world. Hence, it is defined as "esoteric."

Let me say this: the sadhanas of devas are really the dharma protector practices. The inner realization practice is the practice of vital winds, channels and drops. The Tantra Yoga is the practice of purity. The fire offering practice is also the practice of Clear Light. The process of cultivation removes hindrances, increases wisdom, and transforms mundane humans into holy beings. Such powers are incredible!

If you criticize Vajrayana Buddhism, it is as good as criticizing the Tathagata, Vairocana Buddha himself. This is because upon the seventh day of Shakyamuni Buddha's Enlightenment, the Buddha, identified as Vairocana, expounded the doctrines of inner realization in the vast palace of Vajradharmadhatu. This exposition became the *Mahavairocana Sutra*.

21. Ignorance

When the Buddha attained Enlightenment under the Bodhi Tree, he said, "The inherent True Nature of all sentient beings is not different from the Tathagata (Vairocana). All worldly and transcendental merits of sentient beings are therefore already accomplished and completed. Yet it is ignorance that blinds sentient beings from realizing the inherent light and merits within."

Please take note of the word "ignorance." Once ignorance is removed, sentient beings and the Buddha are equal and without any difference.

The cultivation of Vajrayana Buddhism follows the Three Secrets:
the Secret of the Body - Forming mudras;
the Secret of Speech - Chanting mantras;
the Secret of the Mind - Contemplating Right Thoughts (Pure Visualization).

Someone once mentioned, "The practice of Vajrayana Buddhism emphasizes visualization, such as the visualization of offerings which are transformed from a single offering into multiple offerings, filling all space. Since what is visualized is fabricated, and fabrications are discursive thoughts, then offering such fabrications is deceiving the buddhas and bodhisattvas. Isn't this ignorance?"

My reply was, "In order to remove ignorance, it is essential to apply the method of 'ending illusion with illusion.' Hence, you remove discursive thoughts with thoughts, which is attaining reality through the use of illusion.

"Although the visualization of offerings being transformed is a thought process, it is, nevertheless, done with sincerity. Together with the empowerment of mantra recitation and mudra formation, the visualization of offerings is blessed by the power of the Three Secrets of the Tathagata. Such power is incredible, and could actually fulfill every wish you make."

Hence, this is the miraculous transformation of empowerment, which reveals the knowledge of your mind as it really is. To outsiders, everything is fabricated and false. Yet in Vajrayana Buddhism, all fabrications, once blessed by the miraculous transformational power of the Tathagata, are transformed into reality.

People of modern times have come across my propagation of the True Buddha Tantra. Actually, I am True Suchness, and I am the Buddhadharma. Through the application of the Three Secrets of Body, Speech and Mind, a multitude of wonderfully profound and secret dimensions are expressed. If one forgoes the Three Secrets, there can be no hope of attaining buddhahood!

Mantra, mudra, and visualization. Body, speech, and mind. Through gaining spiritual resonance with the Three Secrets, blessings through miraculous transformation, and realizing truth through the use of illusion, one can attain buddhahood in this lifetime.

22. Liberal Validation

Besides receiving validation from your root guru, can the Vajrayana practitioner validate himself, such as that of liberal validation?

I feel that this can only be done by someone who has the correct view of cultivation. Such a practitioner must have actual attainment gained from true practice, and must have great compassion for others. He must thoroughly master the theoretical and practical aspects of cultivation, be wise and humble, and transform his five poisons into the Five Transcendental Wisdoms.

Thus the first few things to validate when exercising liberal validation are:

Is your mind purified? Is your speech purified? Is your body purified?

Do you have sufficient vital wind or qi? Are your channels unblocked? Are you free from the leakage of drops? Have you gained bliss? Has the clear light appeared?

Has your mind been emptied? Have you attained completion of the ground of fruition?

The last validation is, "The doctrines of inner realization attained by the Tathagata cannot be fathomed even by bodhisattvas who have attained the Stage of Equal Enlightenment. It is only known between buddhas."

People today are living in a degenerate age. As such, if liberal validation is advocated, it is difficult to tell the real gurus from the pseudo ones. Many do not speak the truth, and yet they claim to have attained enlightenment when they have not. These pseudo gurus look for quick ways to get rich, coveting fame and fortune, thereby deceiving themselves and others. They put on a cloak of falsehood and try to pass themselves off as the real thing, but in so doing they have stepped onto the evil path and will descend to hell at the end of their lives.

Liberal validation shall result in the following occurrences:

1. A liar claiming he is enlightened.
2. A lunatic (mental patient) also claiming he is enlightened.
3. An individual possessed by mara also claiming he is enlightened.
4. Any person possessed by ghosts claiming he has great spiritual powers.
5. A seemingly highly accomplished adept is actually being fooled by mara.

I feel that it is better to be honest with your cultivation. Do not hold onto thoughts that one has already reached certain spiritual heights and realms.

Be natural, or it will be easy to become attached to illusory forms and run the risk of destroying your "wisdom life" [which means "spiritual life"].

23. Sutrayana and Vajrayana

The Sutrayana tradition is known for its easy to understand doctrines.

The Vajrayana tradition is known for its deep and profound exposition of the inner realized doctrines.

As it is embedded with secret teachings inaccessible to many, it is thus described as "esoteric." It is also defined as an esoteric teaching as it is only taught to those who have taken refuge and have received the required initiation. Otherwise, its doctrines are concealed from the uninitiated.

The Sutrayana and Vajrayana traditions both stem from Shakyamuni Buddha's own teachings of attaining buddhahood. The *Mahavairocana Sutra* states that when the Buddha was enlightened, all buddhas suddenly appeared like sesame seeds filling all space. They praised the revelation of the doctrine of attaining buddhahood, which involves the visualization of the syllable OM seated on a moon disc at the third eye chakra, through which one attains the inherent bodhi within one's heart. What this means is that when Shakyamuni Buddha attained enlightenment, he assumed the identity of Vairocana in the first seven days, and spoke to Vajrasattva and the assembly of holy beings at the vast palace of Vajradharmadhatu. Vairocana, absorbed in a state of Dharma bliss, expounded the doctrines of inner realization which later became the *Mahavairocana Sutra*. Subsequently, at the Palace of the True Word, Vairocana expounded on the Dharma whose doctrines formed the *Vajrasekhara Sutra*. This is the origin of Vajrayana Buddhism.

The lineage of Vajrayana Buddhism arises from Vajrasattva, who personally received the transmission from Vairocana. Hence, Vairocana became the Root Buddha of Vajrayana Buddhism. Vairocana is also known as "The Most Supreme Clear Infinite Eye Treasury Tathagata," who is Buddha Locana.

Let us think of the lineage - Vairocana Tathagata, Buddha Locana, Padmakumara, and finally Living Buddha Lian-sheng. This lineage is thus embedded with such secrets, and I have actually openly revealed my identity in this lineage since the early days. Therefore, True Buddha School as an entity embodies all the secret teachings expounded by every Buddha. The school itself is a great secret.

> **Within *The True Buddha Sutra***
> **The White Lotus Flower is revealed**
> **Expressing spontaneous spiritual powers**
> **While seated on the lion throne**
> **Embodied with compassion and great merits**
> **Expounding the purest Dharma**
> **Receiving praises and admiration**
> **From all buddhas and bodhisattvas**

True Buddha School is founded on the basis of ensuring that the seed of buddhahood shall continue to sprout, tailored to the needs of the world. Thus, its emergence is extraordinary. From now on, one must abide by the instructions given and put them into practice.

24. Dharma Name

The disciples of True Buddha School are addressed with the Dharma name beginning with the word Lian [Chinese for "lotus"]. Lotus, as a symbol, carries multiple meanings:

1. A lotus grows from mud yet is untainted by it, thus representing the stage of moving into buddhahood from the mundane level.
2. With the attainment of fruition, one gains rebirth in Maha Twin Lotus Ponds.
3. Everyone is an emanation of the lotus, and everyone is thus Padmakumara.
4. The world of Maha Twin Lotus Pond is linked to the Flower Adornment World of Shakyamuni Buddha, connected to the Flower Adornment World of Amitabha Buddha, and leads to the Flower Adornment World of Vairocana Tathagata, which is also known as the Secret Adornment World (Mitsugon Kokudo).
5. The lineage guru of Vajrayana Buddhism is Padmasamb-

hava.

6. The root guru of True Buddha School is Lian-sheng (which means "lotus-born").

7. The lineage guru is Lian-sheng, and all the disciples of True Buddha School are addressed as Lotus so and so. This is a collective expression of the Wisdom of Equanimity, the Great Mirror-like Wisdom, the Wisdom of Ultimate Reality, the All-Accomplishing Wisdom, and the Non-Discriminating Wisdom [which leads to the Wisdom of Discriminatory Awareness].

8. When the lineage guru and all his disciples are one and the same, it is called "yoga" or "union" [or spiritual resonance].

9. The wisdom of seeing others as equal to oneself is known as the Wisdom of Equanimity. Sharing the same Dharma name is the most outstanding hallmark of True Buddha School. The meaning of the root guru prostrating to inconceivable sentient beings lies herein. All sentient beings inherently possess Buddha-nature.

10. Only through the cultivation of equanimity shall one attain "no hatred and no enmity," and enter into the realm of "no thought." Thus, one shall realize that "no thought is Buddha."

Here is a verse:

The Perfectly Enlightened Amitabha
Expressed through Lian-sheng as an abbot
The pure lotus assembly of the Tathagata
Shall attain Enlightenment born of the lotus

25. The Secret Referred to in the Secret Teachings

Different gurus hold varying views on the definition of the term "secret," as in the secret teachings of Vajrayana Buddhism. Generally, the views can be summed up as follows:

One view states that since Vajrayana Buddhism mainly hinges on the use of secret mantras, it is therefore defined as the "secret teachings."

Another view suggests that the process of establishing mandalas, reciting mantras, transforming the three karmas of body, speech, and mind into the Three Secrets, shall immediately remove hindrances and increase wisdom, transforming one from mundane existence to buddhahood. Its power is simply incredible, and hence it is called the "secret teachings."

Yet another view says that since Vairocana spoke of the secrets of the Vajradhatu and Garbhadhatu mandalas in the Palace of Vajradharmadhatu, it is thus called the "secret teachings." This teaching is profound, and is usually concealed in deep secrecy. Only few gain access to its teachings. Hence, the term secret is attached to this school of thought.

Ten Mental Abidings are established in Vajrayana Buddhism, of which the first nine are also mentioned in the Sutrayana tradition. However, the last or tenth mental abiding is known as the Secret Adornment Mind. The secret lies in the manifestation of infinite dharmas as expressed through the teachings of the Vajradhatu and Garbhadhatu, the six elements (earth, water, fire, wind, space and consciousness), the Three Secrets and the Five Wisdoms. Such secret Dharmas are unheard of even by bodhisattvas who have attained the level of equal enlightenment, and these doctrines are the very heart of the secret teachings, or Vajrayana Buddhism.

The Vajrayana cultivator relies on the Three Secrets to purify the body, speech and mind. Having been empowered by the Three Secrets of the Tathagata, and eventually becoming one with the Tathagata, it is not necessary for the practitioner to go through cycles of kalpas to attain enlightenment. Once he enters the Dharma Realm [or Dharmadhatu], he attains buddhahood in this very body. This is the secret of the miraculous transformation through the empowerment of Mahayoga.

This is how I personally feel:

The doctrines of Vajrayana Buddhism are divided into many stages, which are established according to the respective inborn faculties [or varying dispositions] of sentient beings. If the teachings are taught indiscriminately to an individual whose inborn faculties do not meet the requirements, the individual may not be able to accept the teachings and in turn may slander them. Thus, the secret doctrines are not revealed to the uninitiated - hence it is a secret.

Moreover, the areas of mantra, mudra and visualization are profound realms that reach far beyond the boundaries of both written and verbal language, their nature of spiritual resonance beyond the understanding of common logic and reasoning. Seen from the perspective of this world, it is difficult to comprehend the teachings. Naturally, such high and profound teachings are secret.

Vajrayana Buddhism's Great Perfection is beyond words and verbalization. It is formless, and unrestricted. Hence, it is even more of a secret.

The True Buddha practitioner must generate the mind for Supreme Enlightenment in his or her cultivation and actions. One must remember that we are not doing this for ourselves, but for the sake of sentient beings, for they always come first.

Sheng-yen Lu

26. Mahabodhicitta, the Mind of Perfect Enlightenment

We are aware that the path of cultivation can take the Hinayana or Mahayana path. The fruition of Hinayana can be classified as the sravaka's enlightenment [hearer] and pratyekabuddha's enlightenment [solitary realizer]. The fruition of Mahayana is Supreme Enlightenment, the highest Perfect Enlightenment attained upon the fruition of buddhahood.

Actually, the generation of Mahabodhicitta is simply the generation of the heart of Supreme Perfect Enlightenment.

Mahabodhicitta is the mind required to follow the way of the bodhisattva: liberating all sentient beings dwelling in the four forms of birth, the six realms of transmigration and the nine states of existence [that sentient beings enjoy dwelling in] so that they may enter into nirvana. This mind is infinite and endless, hence it is termed Mahabodhicitta.

I, Living Buddha Lian-sheng, vow to liberate sentient beings in the Saha world in all my lifetimes, and in so doing I am willing to sacrifice myself completely. If the hells are not empty, I shall not attain buddhahood.

Making a vow like this is Mahabodhicitta. Having made vows, one must also put them into practice.

If someone vows to establish the world's largest religious community, build the world's largest monastery, or form the world's largest charitable organization, the generation of bodhicitta is quite great. But it pales in comparison to the act of liberating beings from the four forms of birth (birth from an egg, such as birds; birth from a womb, such as mammals; birth from moisture or water-born, as with worms and fish; and metamorphic, as with moths from the chrysalis, or with devas, or in the hells, or the first beings in a newly evolved world) and the six realms (deva, human, asura, hell, hungry ghost, and animal) through multiple lifetimes.

The True Buddha practitioner must generate the mind for Supreme Enlightenment in his or her cultivation and actions. One must remember that we are not doing this for ourselves, but for the sake of sentient beings, for they always come first. As for us, we come last. Only then can we reduce the entanglement of karma and attain enlightenment within this lifetime.

On the other hand, if you think in terms of "my territory, my fame and my fortune" - that is anything but Mahabodhicitta. Mahabodhicitta means putting sentient beings before yourself, and certainly not thinking about yourself! So if it isn't Mahabodhicitta, what state of mind is it?

The answer is simple: It is a selfish state of mind.

27. Perfect Penetration of the Sutrayana and Vajrayana Teachings

When I ascended the Dharma throne and expounded the Dharma to an assembly of two thousand lamas at the Drepung Loseling Monastery, I touched on "the Essentials of Vajrayana Cultivation."

When I descended the throne, the khenpo or abbot of the monastery said to me, "What you have just spoken of is beyond their comprehension."

"Why?" I was astonished. The khenpo then explained to me, "The lamas learn only the five sastras [Pramanavartika, Abhisamayalamkara, Madhamakavatara, Vinaya and Abhidharmakosha] of the Sutrayana tradition while studying here in the three major monasteries. Upon completion of their education, they then proceed to either the Upper Tantric College or Lower Tantric College, or other Tantric grwa tshang (college) to learn the Vajrayana teachings."

His explanation certainly enlightened me. Cultivation of Tibetan Buddhism requires you to study the Buddhadharma of the Sutrayana tradition for twelve years, following which you must spend another eight years cultivating according to the Tantra teachings. All in all, it takes twenty years of education before you gain a thorough understanding of the Sutrayana and Vajrayana teachings.

It goes without saying that the Vajrayana doctrines are indeed very precious. In the past, when a person wished to receive the transmission of a practice, he was required to make an offering of all his wealth, climb mountains and cross rivers, or take a long and hazardous journey before he could receive the empowerment. Today, with the wide propagation of the True Buddha Tantra, we ought to treasure this opportunity offered to us to learn the Buddhadharma.

As Vajrayana practitioners, we should know that two schools of thought exist in Buddhism, the Sutrayana and the Vajrayana traditions. The Sutrayana tradition tends to focus more on principle, whereas the Vajrayana tradition focuses more on practice to reach enlightenment. The Sutrayana tradition offers the basic teaching of Buddhism, and it is important to learn the teachings of both traditions. When practicing the Vajrayana teachings, you need to brush up on the theoretical aspects of Buddhism. Grounded with the proper views of Buddhism, you will not go astray while studying Vajrayana Buddhism.

True Buddha School advocates the perfect interpenetration of the Sutrayana and Vajrayana teachings, though we begin with the Vajrayana practices. When I deliver my dharma talks, I place great emphasis on Tsongkhapa's *The Great Treatise on the Stages of the Path to Enlightenment* [Lamrim Chenmo] and *The Great Exposition of Secret Mantra* [sNgag-rim chenmo].

If the Sutrayana tradition is the shirt, then the Vajrayana tradition is the collar. There is no way you can forgo the shirt and wear only the collar.

28. The Mandala

Whenever a practice is expounded in Vajrayana Buddhism, establishing a mandala is required. This stage thus involves the establishment of a mandala, the recitation of mantras and the cultivation of a sadhana. Before the start of the exposition on *The Great Exposition of Secret Mantra* [sNgag-rim chenmo], a mandala (shrine) is first established.

Someone once told me, "The mandala is false. It is merely a facade!"

I replied, "The mandala is built for the purposes of making offerings, cultivation, recitation, adornment, and providing a sense of direction. All Vajrayana empowerments must be carried out within a mandala."

I explained in further detail, "Upon the construction of the square and round symmetries of the mandala, the respective deities are positioned within for our worship. The assembly of the deities forms the essence of the mandala. Hence, the mandala is the gathering place of the deities. Besides, it functions as a basis for chanting and being so, transcends into a focal point where all merits converge."

It is stated in the *Mahavairocana Sutra* that the great compassionate perfections numbering as many as the specks of dust from the worlds of the ten directions are like the Flower Treasury. And the infinite emanation bodies spanning the Three Vehicles and the six realms are the leaves, the stem and the roots. All of them are illuminating light together, displaying a perfect and complete matrix of merits which is called the mandala.

I honestly told the questioner the following truth:

The reality of buddhas abiding in space is itself a secret. However, the presence of a mandala is an expedient means. The practitioner, through expedient cultivation practices, enters the mandala through the Dharma current of the buddhas, and receives the empowerment from within. Hence, the space, the mandala and the practitioner form the three stages of reality-realms. This is the true doctrine of Vajrayana Buddhism.

Through the application of the three secret expedient means, we give empowerment to sentient beings, nurturing their Buddha-nature. You say the mandala is false! That it is merely a facade! But I say it is not, that it only functions as an expedient means. Today, I hold the true merits of the Tathagatas within me, and with the lights and Dharma currents of all deities numbering as many as the specks of dust in the worlds of the ten directions converging upon me, I shall empower all sentient beings and help them attain the supreme mind of Vairocana.

Contemplate it! Contemplate it! The very essence of Perfect Enlightenment is simply pure and wonderful.

29. Attaining Buddhahood in This Very Body

Many students of Buddhism, upon studying the Sutrayana teachings, insist that it would take as long as three Asankhya kalpas to attain buddhahood. A small kalpa is represented as 16,798,000 years, and twenty small kalpas add up to a middle kalpa. Four middle kalpas form a mahakalpa, which is 1,343,840,000 years. Hence, three Asankhya kalpas literally represent innumerable and unimaginable eons.

Therefore, these students of Buddhism do not agree with the Vajrayana Buddhist view that one can attain buddhahood in this very body. But please read what is explicitly expounded in the "Breakthrough Sermon" [by Bodhidharma]:

Student: "But the Buddha said, 'Only after undergoing innumerable hardships for three Asankhya kalpas did I achieve enlightenment.' Why do you now say that simply beholding the mind and overcoming the three poisons is liberation?"

Bodhidharma: "The words of the Buddha are true, but the three

Asankhya kalpas refer to the three poisoned states of mind. What we call Asankhya in Sanskrit you call countless. Within these three poisoned states of mind are countless evil thoughts, and every thought lasts a kalpa. Such infinity is what the Buddha meant by the three Asankhya kalpas. Once the three poisons obscure your real self, how can you be called liberated until you overcome your countless evil thoughts? People who can transform the three poisons of greed, anger, and ignorance into the three liberations are said to pass through the three Asankhya kalpas. But people of this final age are the densest of beings. They don't understand what the Tathagata really meant by the three Asankhya kalpas. They say enlightenment is only achieved after endless kalpas and thereby mislead disciples to retreat from the path to buddhahood."

This explains how the three Asankhya kalpas actually refer to the countless thoughts generated by the three poisons. Every thought lasts a kalpa. Thus, countless thoughts are transformed into countless kalpas as numerous as the grains of sand in the Ganges River.

To attain buddhahood in this very body, one only needs to remove the three poisons and instantly one shall transcend the three Asankhya kalpas, and attain buddhahood.

Why is attaining buddhahood in this very body possible with Vajrayana Buddhism? My view is:

1. Buddha and I have become One (the Nirmanakaya Emanation Body).
2. Empowerment through Miraculous Transformation (the Sambhogakaya Bliss Body).
3. The Nature of Emptiness of the Dharma Realm (the Dharmakaya Truth Body).

When one cultivates accordingly, one reaches attainment accordingly. Vajrayana Buddhism involves the cultivation and attainment of the Emanation Body, Bliss Body and Truth Body. Thus, the attainment of buddhahood in this very body is achievable.

In truth, all Vajrayana practitioners who have not reached the level of spirituality attained by the lineage gurus must abide by the Five Precepts and the Ten Virtues, which are set as the essential disciplinary codes of Buddhism.

Sheng-yen Lu

30. Refrain from Killing

A Vajrayana lineage guru was fishing by the riverside. A young boy approached him and asked, "The Buddhist precepts say not to kill. So why do you kill?"

The guru turned around and looked at the boy, started laughing, and said, "You were once fished by me."

Padmasambhava once killed all the robbers, bandits and vicious killers living in the Butcher City who had committed murder and arson, and then employed the most compassionate deliverance practice to purify their spirits, and sent them to the Western Paradise of Ultimate Bliss instantaneously.

In these two examples, it would appear that the Vajrayana gurus were killing living beings. But in actual fact, they were exercising the most compassionate means of deliverance. Their intention was not to kill, but to deliver. This really is true salvation and deliverance for the people of the world.

My analysis of this situation is as follows:

The Sutrayana tradition teaches non-killing, and encourages the deliverance of life. Hence, the protection of animal life is in keeping with this sense of compassion, which grows with such acts of benevolence. However, the so-called killings carried out by Vajrayana gurus are in reality the deliverance of sentient beings, touching the spiritual level with a deeper compassion, liberating and purifying them so that their spirits may seek rebirth in the Buddha Pure Land.

In truth, all Vajrayana practitioners who have not reached the level of spirituality attained by the lineage gurus must abide by the Five Precepts and the Ten Virtues, which are set as the essential disciplinary codes of Buddhism. If one can perform the act of killing followed by deliverance, one's spiritual attainment is equal to the Tathagata in the Dharmakaya Truth Body, whose ground of fruition is perfect and complete, and as such, can draw sentient beings to itself by incredible means!

Today's Vajrayana practitioners barely scratch the surface of the Vajrayana doctrines. Far from reaching the stage of buddhahood, their behavior shows great lack of discipline and displays a lack of kindness towards others. Hence, while it is harmless to know of a practice such as deliverance through killing, they should never use it under any circumstances. Instead of helping to deliver any spirits, they would bring harm to Vajrayana Buddhism and its teachings. Be careful! Be careful!

31. Eating Meat or Vegetarian Meals

Someone once asked the Dalai Lama, "What is Vajrayana Buddhism's stand on vegetarianism and meat eating?"

The Dalai Lama replied, "I personally am a vegetarian, but other lamas aren't." The questioner then raised this issue, "If a person is not a vegetarian, then he or she is killing. Isn't this a breach of the Five Precepts?"

The reply given by the Dalai Lama was ambiguous, suggesting that being non-vegetarian does not imply one is killing, and that killing has nothing to do with being vegetarian. In fact, the Dalai Lama laughed embarrassingly and said, "Lamas don't kill for food, but they are not vegetarians."

When I was at Drepung Loseling Monastery having a meal with the khenpo [or abbot], only meat was served. As far as I know, the Buddhists in China received a decree from Xiaoyan, the Chinese Emperor Wu of the Liang Dynasty, to instruct their ordained monks and nuns to adopt a vegetarian lifestyle. This is a special characteristic of Chinese Buddhism, which has the intention to nurture compassion and avoid creating negative karma.

Consuming vegetarian meals in itself has its merits, but it is not a major factor to attaining buddhahood. If being vegetarian by itself could lead to buddhahood, horses, cows and sheep would be well on their way to attaining enlightenment!

Many beginners in Buddhism are not accustomed to sticking to a vegetarian lifestyle. It is advisable that they consume what is called the "three pure meats" (not personally witnessing the animal being killed, not personally hearing of its cry while it is being killed, and when the animal was not specifically killed for the person eating it). This is a convenient solution as an alternative to adopting a vegetarian lifestyle.

Should a True Buddha practitioner adopt a strict vegetarian life-style? My answer to this is: "It's up to you." But any meat-eating prac-titioner must purify their meat by "blowing a gust of air" and recit-ing the Manjushri Deliverance Mantra. This is applying the Vajrayana methods to deliver the spirits of the animals, and transforming the meat into purified food. Upon offering merits to the spirit of the ani-mal whose meat is to be consumed, the meat can thus be eaten. This is because when you have extended your compassion and delivered the spirit, there exists no bond of negative karmic affinity between you and the animal's spirit.

The views held by Sutrayana and Vajrayana Buddhism on eating meat and vegetarian meals are different, but please remember this verse expounded by the Buddha:

> **One mouthful of pure water**
> **Contains eighty four thousand worms**
> **If you do not recite a deliverance mantra**
> **It is as good as killing**

Such subtle truth must be discerned carefully!

32. Offering Wine and Meat to the Buddha

When the head of the Gelug order of Tibetan Buddhism, His Holiness Ganden Tripa, visited Seattle Leizang Temple in Redmond [in September, 1996], he gave me a Dharma robe as a gift. During his visit, it coincided with the birthday of a Vajra Buddha whom His Holiness worshipped. His Holiness then requested that the monks of Seattle Leizang Temple help him purchase a bottle of wine and some beef and lamb meat from the supermarket. He wanted to cultivate and make an offering to the Vajra Buddha.

Later, a monk asked me in private, "Can we offer wine and meat to the buddhas?" I explained to the monk that in the view of the Sutrayana tradition, drinking wine and taking meat would have breached the precepts, but this is not the case according to Vajrayana teachings. The view of Vajrayana Buddhism is that all buddhas are beings abiding in the mind of non-discrimination. Therefore, in the eyes of the buddhas, wine and meat are not seen as wine and meat. For example, in the eyes of men, wine is wine. In the eyes of the asuras, wine is a sword and a knife. To the hungry ghosts, wine becomes a burning flame. The hell beings see wine manifested as a pool of blood. Yet, to the buddhas, wine is fine nectar.

Let me say this:

If the practitioner is pure, the wine and meat consumed become pure. Hence the very act of consuming wine and meat is pure. On the contrary, if the practitioner is impure, the wine and meat consumed become impure. Hence, the very act of consuming wine and meat is impure. Please think through this carefully and discern the truth!

A practitioner with actual attainment will transform the wine into nectar, and the meat into cleansed food. As he delivers the spirits of the slaughtered animals, there is no danger of misbehavior in consuming wine and meat.

A practitioner who has no spiritual stamina will drink wine until he is drunk, and consume meat out of gluttony. He has breached a major precept in Vajrayana Buddhism, and has created heavy karma for himself, which would draw him to the Vajra Hell upon his death.

On the surface, both scenarios may appear similar, but they are separated by the polarities of purity and impurity!

I feel that it is equal and undifferentiated to offer either vegetarian meals or meat to the buddhas. But should you want to consume wine and meat, you must know where your spiritual stamina stands. If one is corrupted by the consumption of meat and wine, then it is absolutely necessary to strictly follow the precepts and refrain from consuming wine and meat!

33. Why Practice Buddhism and Do Cultivation?

Having written many articles on the "Insights of the Tathagata," I am back to the starting point, addressing the issue: Why practice Buddhism and do cultivation?

Why practice Buddhism? Why is there a need to cultivate? Such questions may not even arise in the minds of many who feel that the goal of being alive as a human is simply staying alive, and upon your death everything ends. These people see no reason to make their lives more difficult by being tied down with the practice of Buddhism.

Someone asked me, "When it is time to party, I party. Why should I bother learning Buddhism? Why stick to precepts?" Others have added, "I have no desire to become a buddha or bodhisattva. So why bother to cultivate?" Another person said, "Religious stuff is crap! It is just pure nonsense! Cause and effect, heaven and hell... I don't believe any of it."

We need to exercise greater patience when explaining the teachings to these individuals, offering them some introductory literature on Buddhism as gifts.

I would share with them my understanding and realization. It is my view that human life is a cycle of suffering involving birth, old age, sickness and death. Hence, suffering, emptiness and impermanence always exist. When I look into the true meaning of life, I realize that the joy in it is short-lived, for life is short. Life is also illusory like a dream, so therefore it would be wise to penetrate beyond our present vision of life and resolve the question of life and death.

Just think of the impermanence of the events in life, and how fragile life is. Contemplate on the true meaning of our existence, and why our hearts remain empty. Think of how one can gain all the treasures and achievements of the world, only to lose it all upon death. What joy can these treasures bring?

With such awareness comes a sense of alertness! I genuinely realized that the utmost value in our short lifetime on earth is to practice cultivation with perseverance, attaining true liberation, self-realization, and spiritual freedom. Otherwise, everything else is simply trash generated from discursive thoughts!

34. The Guru's Power of Blessing

A certain story is widespread in Tibet, and it goes like this:
A lama climbed up a huge tree where a beehive was found. The bees were buzzing around the lama, but the lama whispered to the bees, "Don't sting me!" And interestingly, the bees ignored the lama and did not sting him at all!

Another lama who saw this was very puzzled, and wanted to know the secret of avoiding being stung by the bees. The lama who was not stung by the bees revealed that there was no secret to this except that he just told the bees not to sting him. The curious lama then climbed up the tree and said the same thing to the bees, "Don't sting me!" However, the bees ignored his words and swarmed towards the curious lama and stung him fiercely. The poor lama screamed and begged for his life.

Why is it that the same words would bring different results? It is said that the first lama prayed to his guru for a blessing before climbing the tree, resulting in the bees listening to him, whereas the second lama followed the instruction without first seeking a blessing from his guru, thus ending up being stung.

The names of buddhas mentioned in the sutras of the Sutrayana tradition are available for recitation to anyone who comes across them. There are no restrictions over this chanting. But Vajrayana Buddhism approaches this differently. The practice texts of Vajrayana Buddhism are printed with the notice, "Please do not read the text without first receiving the proper empowerment." It is required that before the recitation of Vajrayana mantras, you must first receive the proper empowerment and blessing from your master. Otherwise, all chanting is void and fruitless, and it is an act of "dharma theft," which is a breach of the Samaya Pledge. Under this situation, you would never be able to generate the dharma power of spiritual resonance through the cultivation of mantra chanting.

Hence, it is only by taking refuge, receiving empowerment, and gaining the blessings of your guru that cultivation can be authorized. Only then can the inherent Buddha-nature emerge from delusions, topsy-turvy events, discursive thoughts and attachments.

The guru's power of blessing is the very key to attaining accomplishment through Vajrayana cultivation!

35. The Precious Teachings of Vajrayana Buddhism

In the past, Vairocana Buddha transmitted the supreme vehicle of Unexcelled Yoga secretly to Vajrasattva, who waited hundreds of years before transmitting the same doctrines to Nagarjuna Bodhisattva. Nagarjuna waited another several hundred years before transmitting the secret doctrines to Acharya Nagabodhi, who in turn waited several centuries before transmitting the teachings to Acharya Vajrabodhi. Vajrabodhi then proceeded to the east and arrived in China, transmitting the secret teachings to two senior monks, Amoghavajra and Zen Master Yixing.

Hence, from the Tathagata to the senior monks in China, the Vajrayana Buddhist teachings were directly transmitted to only six acharyas or gurus. Therefore, the Vajrayana doctrines are very precious.

The Essentials of Vajrayana Buddhism states: "Vajrayana Buddhism is the supreme wisdom gained upon self-realization by the Buddha, whose doctrines are transmitted directly to ordinary people entangled in the mundane world. As such, when one cultivates these doctrines, one receives swift progress in which the power attained is simply unimaginable. However, the Vajrayana teachings place great emphasis on sadhanas, and those who wish to practice must enter the great mandala and receive the empowerment from the vajra master before they can be allowed to cultivate the practice. Otherwise, it would be considered an act of dharma theft, drawing upon oneself unthinkable negative karmic consequences. Thus in China, Vajrayana Buddhism has been lost since the Tang and Song dynasties, for no one would dare to study it."

From this, we know that the self-realized holy wisdom of the Tathagata is extremely precious indeed!

The fact that "no one would dare to study it" is itself shocking. The fact that swift progress can be attained in Vajrayana Buddhism, with the power gained far surpassing that of other schools, has attracted great interest and attention to its doctrines.

Shakyamuni Buddha once used the five stages of making ghee [pancaksira, or refined cream] to represent the five respective canons:

Milk is the Sutra canon
Cream is the Vinaya canon
Fresh butter is the Abhidharma canon
Melted butter is the Prajna canon
Ghee is the Vajrayana canon

Ghee is the very essence of milk, and hence, Vajrayana Buddhism embodies the essence of the Buddhadharma. It is said that if one leaves Vajrayana Buddhism, there can be no hope of attaining buddhahood.

It is rare for one to hear the Vajrayana doctrines. You should be glad that you have found them this time.

36. The Jambhala or Wealth Deity Practice

Someone once asked me, "Wealth, lust, fame, eating and sleep-
ing are the major desires of humans. They are known as the five
roots of hell. Yet why is the Jambhala Practice included in Vajrayana
Buddhism?"

I replied, "Vajrayana Buddhism, in its mission to deliver sentient
beings, is aware that sentient beings love wealth. Hence, projecting
the extensive field of compassionate vows, it exercises the approach of
first attracting sentient beings through desire, and later leading them
into the wisdom of the Buddha."

Question: How do you approach the wisdom of the Buddha
through the Jambhala Practice?

Answer: The cultivation of the Jambhala Practice will also lead to
the experience of Dharma taste, resulting in a natural transformation
of desire. Eventually, it leads to a transformation of consciousness into
wisdom, reaching a level of attainment.

Question: What kinds of Jambhala practices are there in Vajrayana
Buddhism?

Answer: There are the practices of the Yellow Jambhala, Red Jambhala, Green Jambhala, Black Jambhala, White Jambhala, and the Five Wealth Deities. In addition, the Dragon Treasure Vase Practice, Earth Deity Practice, Mountain God Practice and so forth are all wealth deity practices.

Question: When cultivating the wealth deity practices, what are the prerequisites to achieving spiritual resonance?

Answer: To achieve spiritual resonance and results during cultivation, one must generate bodhicitta such that upon receiving massive wealth, one gives away alms and vows to do more charities. Hence, with the expansion of your bodhicitta, blessings and merits shall increase continuously. These acts of generosity shall transform greed into the purity of compassion.

Question: Which of the Jambhala Practices in Vajrayana Buddhism is the best method?

Answer: They are the same. As long as you achieve spiritual resonance, that would be the best Jambhala Practice.

My view is that the very spirit presented in the Jambhala Practice is the spirit of relinquishment. To relinquish is to receive, and in giving one gains: the amount you may receive corresponds with the amount you are willing to let go. Hence, once you relinquish all, you would naturally receive everything. For example, if you hold onto something in your hand and are not willing to release it, then how could you receive another more precious gift that may come your way?

The Dharma taste of receiving and losing thus lies in the practice.

37. The Wrathful Vajra Protectors

Vajra protectors are divine beings that hold vajra implements in their hands and protect the Buddhadharma. These vajra protectors are called "instructional wheels," which symbolize the great strength of the instruction, and can destroy all forms of enemies.

In the Chinese Sutrayana tradition, the common dharma protectors that protect the Buddhadharma are Sangharama [Qielan] and Skanda [Weituo]. In Vajrayana Buddhism, the wrathful vajra protectors are very distinctive in their appearance, and they are the emanation bodies of buddhas and bodhisattvas. Isn't it true that Buddhism teaches you to avoid anger and to practice patience? Then why do they appear to be so ferocious?

There is a saying in Buddhism, which states:

The bodhisattvas lower their eyebrows, showering compassion on the six realms. The vajra protectors stare with angry eyes, subjugating the four maras.

While remaining compassionate within, the buddhas and bodhisattvas, in their efforts to subjugate and deliver the mara devas, vicious deities, evil ghosts, yaksas, and malicious people who are extremely unreasonable, manifest an external aspect of wrathfulness to subdue these beings so that they may take refuge in the Buddha.

The wrathful vajra protectors in Tibetan Buddhism are unique, and exist for very special reasons. In the early days, the Bon religion was widespread in Tibet, and the worship of nature prevailed. People worshiped the mountains, fire, bulls, horses, pigs, snakes, etc.

Then, Manjushri Bodhisattva entered samadhi and manifested Yamantaka (appearing with the head of a bull) to instruct the Tibetans.

Avalokitesvara Bodhisattva entered into samadhi and manifested Hayagriva (appearing with the head of a horse) to instruct the Tibetans.

Vairocana entered samadhi and manifested Vajravarahi (appearing with the head of a sow, or female pig) to instruct the Tibetans.

A lineage guru entered samadhi and manifested Rahula (appearing with the body of a snake) to instruct the Tibetans. And there were others.

Many of these wrathful vajra protectors are found in Tibetan Buddhism. They are the compassionate emanations of the buddhas, bodhisattvas and gurus to liberate sentient beings utilizing an expedient approach.

When a Vajrayana practitioner cultivates the five heruka practices and achieves spiritual resonance, he or she is near the level of buddhahood. The heruka practices of Vajrayana are indeed wonderful and profound.

38. Yab-Yum, the Consort Practice

There exist three unique practices in Vajrayana Buddhism, which are:

1. The Jambhala Practice.
2. The Heruka Practice.
3. The Yab-Yam or Consort Practice.

The Consort Practice, in particular, leaves most people perplexed and puzzled. Isn't it true that Buddhism forbids lascivious sexual acts? Why does the Consort Practice have any presence in the teachings?

The Consort Practice originated in India. The Indian people mature at an early age, and their desire for sex is often great. The Vajrayana gurus had responded according to the nature of sentient beings and designed the Consort Practice as an expedient means to reach them and liberate them.

It is established on the very principle expounded by Vimalakirti when he said: "Without cutting off lust, anger and ignorance and yet not being part of these." This is the expedient approach of "first attracting sentient beings through desire, and later leading them into the wisdom of the Buddha."

The principle establishes that the union of two individuals can be used as a form of cultivation, through which wisdom is produced. And with wisdom one can see through the illusion of sexual lust, by which desire is cut-off, and one is helped to attain purity, transforming desire into emptiness. And through emptiness one attains innate wisdom. The Consort Practice, if cultivated in accordance with this principle, undoubtedly leads to Supreme Purity.

Non-leakage. Emptiness. Bliss. Purity. These are all found within the context of this practice.

The Consort Practice is what Padmasambhava described as "Extracting the pearl from the mouth of the poisonous snake." If one does not cultivate the Consort Practice according to the highest principle, and is not equipped with the proper techniques, it shall result in wrongful cultivation, and the cultivator will easily descend to Vajra Hell. Therefore, it is the most dangerous cultivation practice, and we must certainly be cautioned!

The Consort Practice is most susceptible to slander and criticism. Likewise, Padmasambhava was smeared by his friend, Golden Light Youth and Bhasadhara (Padmasambhava's wife)!

Many of the techniques taught in this practice have long been lost. As the practice is shocking to most people and is easily misunderstood by the uninitiated, it is best to avoid practicing it. (Tsongkhapa himself only practiced with a visualized consort, a Jnana Mudra.)

39. The Fundamental Rationale of Vajrayana Buddhism

I personally find that the fundamental rationales of the Vajrayana tradition and the Sutrayana tradition are completely different. I can tell that the approach employed by the Sutrayana tradition to deliver sentient beings is analogous to the method once used by an ancient Chinese man called Gun, who tried to control a flood by blocking it. However, the approach that Vajrayana Buddhism takes to liberate sentient beings is like the method employed by Gun's son, Yu, who controlled a flood by channeling the water.

These approaches of blocking and channeling are meant to deal with the three poisons of greed, anger and ignorance. Both the Sutrayana and Vajrayana Buddhist traditions acknowledge the presence of these three poisons in the hearts of humans, existing as the accumulated karmic residue from past lives. While the Sutrayana tradition takes the approach of removing these poisons, Vajrayana Buddhism cultivates by coexisting with greed, anger and ignorance.

I have highlighted:

Greed - The Jambhala Practice

Anger - The Heruka Practice
Ignorance - The Consort Practice
This is the fundamental rationale of Vajrayana Buddhism, of which the divine deities can be addressed directly as "Greedy Buddha," "Angry Guardian," "Ignorant Bodhisattva" or "Desirous Bodhisattva."

The rationale of Vajrayana Buddhism is that coexisting with greed, anger and ignorance, which satisfies the wishes of sentient beings through the methods of cultivation, proves to be the most effective approach. Once a practitioner attains the Dharma taste, he or she will naturally understand that greed is emptiness, anger is compassion, and ignorance is wisdom. Eventually, by means of transformation, one realizes there is nothing to gain or lose, and therefore achieves the subjugation of the ego or self. The practitioner sees through the illusion of lust, eventually gaining spirituality upliftment, and attains the innate Buddha wisdom.

Vajrayana Buddhism regards lust, anger and ignorance as aspects of the Buddhadharma, thus it liberates sentient beings accordingly, based on their respective basic instincts and natures. Furthermore, the Vajrayana mantras are able to block all evils, prevent them from arising and arrest any evil actions. It is through such superior wisdom that the fundamental rationale is established. Vajrayana mantras can transform all impurities into purity.

Many people today have little understanding of the fundamental rationale of Vajrayana Buddhism, and they barely scratch the surface of its teachings. They commonly associate Vajrayana Buddhism with things related to strange, mystical, cult-like activities, which engage in the use of spells, wine and meat.

But seriously speaking, the rationale of Vajrayana Buddhism ultimately aims to transform all defilements so then there are no defilements, aiming to purify your mind, and attain supreme purity.

40. Heart Essence and Oral Transmissions

The cultivation of Vajrayana Buddhism is divided into the Generation Stage and the Completion Stage. These stages are clearly defined in their progressive steps. In Vajrayana Buddhism, we must receive empowerment and cultivate according to the respective stages; otherwise, it would be dangerous. This is because as one gains greater attainment in Vajrayana, greater dangers are involved.

I feel that the Vajrayana practitioner should begin with the practice of purifying your body, speech, and mind. Following which, you should cultivate the vital winds, channels and drops. And through the stages of cultivation, you reach the Highest Yoga Tantra and finally the Great Perfection.

The stages of Mahamudra practice in the Kagyu School of Tibetan Buddhism are:

The Yoga of One-pointedness
The Yoga of Simplicity
The Yoga of One Taste
The Yoga of Non-Meditation

The detailed division of the stages includes: the Four Preliminary

Practices, Guru Yoga, Deity Yoga, Vase Breathing Practice, Inner Fire Yoga, the Yoga of Drops, the Yoga of Non-leakage, the Opening of the Five Chakras, Heruka Deity Practice, Highest Yoga Tantra, and the Great Perfection.

Although it is possible to try to cultivate the sadhanas or methods of Vajrayana Buddhism by following the practice texts, their deepest heart essence and oral transmissions are never revealed in the practice texts. They must be transmitted orally by the guru to the disciple, and they are not told to outsiders. Thus, a sutra states, "The secrets of all Vajrayana practices must be transmitted personally by a master, or there can be no attainment."

For example: Only through the guidance of the guru can one understand the secrets of channeling the vital winds into the central channel.

The techniques of the non-leakage practice of the Sakya Six-Limbed sadhana must be practiced with the secret instructions revealed by the guru so that the timely validation of your progress can be ascertained.

How do you regulate the lowering, raising, retaining, and dispersing of drops? Without the oral transmission of a guru, there can be no progress. This is also the case for the technique of "raising the drops and leaping over Mt. Sumeru," where the guru must demonstrate the yoga postures personally. And likewise with all other transmissions.

If a practitioner disregards the heart essence and pith instructions of the guru, he or she will have no idea what the keys are, and would not know how to progress. How can he or she achieve spiritual resonance? Like a blind man walking along the verge of a cliff, it can only mean danger.

The heart essence and oral transmission of Vajrayana Buddhism are extremely profound secrets. Vajrayana practitioners must be cautious!

41. Cultivating with Contemplation and Visualization

During the founding days of Buddhism, Shakyamuni Buddha placed the greatest emphasis on the practice of contemplation. The disciples entered into caves and sat in meditation and contemplated. I once visited both Venerable Ananda's and Venerable Sariputra's caves at Vulture Peak Mountain in India. The caves where the Vajrayana gurus, Naropa and Padmasambhava, once cultivated somehow harmonize better with the Chinese teachings of feng shui. They illuminate brilliantly, and streams of pure Dharma milk flow from them, nurturing all of the Dharma Realms.

There are many contemplative practices in Buddhism, which include the Breath Counting Exercise, Contemplation on Impurity, the Skeleton Visualization Method, the Consciousness-Only Contemplation, Contemplation on the Dharma Realms, Visualization on the Sixteen Meditations of the Pure Land, the Three Modes of Contemplation of the Tiantai School, and so on.

When reciting a mantra, the Vajrayana practitioner must chant along by visualizing:

1. The perfect form of the deity.
2. The seed syllable of the deity.
3. Becoming the deity himself.
4. The seed syllable on the moon disc within your heart.
5. The moon disc within your heart lined with the mantra.

Vajrayana Buddhism places great importance on mantra, mudra and visualization. Among the visualization practices [common in Shingon Buddhism] are the Five Forms Body Transformation Contemplation [Gosōjōjingan], the Five Syllables Contemplation [Gojigonjingan], the Merging of Self and Deity Contemplation [Ruwo-Woru or "nyūga ga'nyū"], the Moon Disc Visualization [Gachirinkan], and the Visualization of the Seed Syllable AH [Ajikan].

I have realized that there is no single object alone in this world which can be used to symbolize bodhicitta. Eventually, the pure and perfect appearance of the moon disc became its symbol. Through the teachings of Vajrayana, you are taught how to form the Vajra-bandha mudra and visualize the heart as a full moon disc appearing pure and clear, displaying a limpid quality throughout. It is characterized by utmost serenity, unmatched by anything in the world. The practitioner abides calmly in stillness, becomes one with the moon disc and finds the brilliance of light radiating through billions of cosmic worlds.

With this practice, your discursive thoughts shall not arise, and the body and mind shall also attain a state of purity, thereby strengthening the great bodhicitta.

Thus, it is:

> **The moon disc within one's heart**
> **Radiates a light of purity**
> **The meditative wisdom is projected into the gesture of Vajra-bandha**
> **And one is drawn into the calm wisdom of the Tathagata**

42. Ajikan, the Visualization of the Seed Syllable AH

Once, my master told me, "There is a very important visualization technique." I asked my master what it was, to which he replied, "It is the visualization of the seed syllable AH. It encompasses the Three Secrets of forming the mudra, chanting the mantra, and contemplating the unborn state of the seed syllable AH."

"What do you mean that the seed syllable AH is unborn?" I asked. My master replied, "It means liberation from life and death, where one no longer needs to be reborn in the Three Realms [of the Desire, Form, and Formless realms] and the six realms of transmigration, abiding constantly in the state of non-creation and non-annihilation within the realm of Maha Nirvana."

The practitioner sits properly in a straight posture and faces a scroll on which is painted a white illuminating moon disc. Inside the disc is an eight-petalled lotus. Resting on the lotus is the seed syllable AH in either Sanskrit or Tibetan script. The practitioner inhales and exhales the seed syllable AH in his or her every breath, and chants the AH seed syllable. When he cultivates in this fashion over a period of time, he should see results. As his cultivation ripens, he should be able to see the moon disc with the syllable AH distinctively, whether his eyes are open or closed. He would need to draw the AH seed syllable moon disc into himself, and at this point, the external AH seed syllable moon disc merges with the syllable AH moon disc within him.

When one gains success with this visualization, one instantly attains buddhahood in this very body and cuts the mistaken view that a duality exists between the concepts of affliction and bodhi, samsara and nirvana.

My Master said, "The name of Amitabha Buddha ranks supreme among all the buddhas of the ten directions and three times because of the syllable AH. This syllable is the common seed syllable of all buddhas and bodhisattvas. Thus, if a person aspires to be reborn in the Western Pure Land, that person only needs to cultivate the visualization of the seed syllable AH to ensure such a rebirth."

From what I know, Shakyamuni Buddha said that all sentient beings have Buddha-nature within their heart, pointing to the existence of a seed of attaining buddhahood. But the Tathagata did not reveal what this seed is.

In Vajrayana Buddhism, this seed is the syllable AH. If the practitioner visualizes the syllable AH with his mind, he would undoubtedly speed his way to buddhahood at a pace that allows him to attain it in this very body. It would far exceed the pace of attaining buddhahood through studying thousands of sutras.

Here lies the very essence and secret of Vajrayana, where the great spiritual resonance of yoga can be found, and through which the very taste of buddhahood is experienced.

43. Choosing One's Personal Deity (Yidam)

My disciples often asked me this question, "Who among the buddhas and bodhisattvas is my personal deity?" [Editor's note: personal deity is also called yidam and meditational deity.]

My reply is, "Yidam, or personal deity, means what is principally the most supreme. From among the buddhas and bodhisattvas, the practitioner will choose a deity who is connected to the individual through many lifetimes. That would be his personal deity."

I added, "A personal deity is determined when the individual feels there is a special affinity between them, where the connection, the affection and the respect for the deity is most pronounced."

In Vajrayana Buddhism, the practice of selecting your personal deity involves a method in which the practitioner is first blindfolded. While holding a flower in his hand, he is led by his guru to the mandala where he casts the flower towards it. His personal deity is determined by the deity upon which the flower lands. In the past, when Master Kukai [or Kobo Daishi, founder of Shingon Buddhism] cast his flower, it landed on Vairocana. His religious name was thus Henjo Kongo, meaning "Universally Illuminating Vajra."

Nowadays, many disciples request help from their root guru to determine their personal deity. The root guru must ascertain the affinity between the disciple and the respective deity to determine their compatibility. If they are compatible, that would surely be the personal deity.

Some disciples who just took refuge and received the refuge empowerment saw the appearance of a buddha or bodhisattva touching their heads and blessing them either in their dreams or meditation. Hence, they would choose that particular buddha or bodhisattva as their personal deity. This is reasonable.

A question was asked, "Can we have two or three personal deities?"

Answer: "In principle, there should be one personal deity. But under special circumstances, one may have two, or even three personal deities."

Question: "If we are uncomfortable with the personal deity, can we change to another?"

Answer: "Actually, it is not advisable to change your personal deity once you have made your decision. As long as you practice earnestly and reach for perfection, you shall achieve spiritual resonance. The truth is that there are no barriers between buddhas and bodhisattvas. Therefore we must hold thoughts of non-differentiation and respect all as equal."

Question: "There are eight major personal deities in True Buddha School. Can we choose a deity outside of these eight?"

Answer: "The group of eight major personal deities is simply a framework. Other deities that exist in the Vajradhatu and Garbhadhatu Mandalas can also be selected as your personal deity."

When I select the personal deity for my disciples, there's a secret involved. I choose the personal deity based on the disciple's "inherent qualities."

44. The Fourfold and Sixfold Refuge

When taking refuge, the Sutrayana tradition practices the Threefold Refuge, in which one takes refuge in the Buddha, the Dharma, and the Sangha. The act of taking refuge is the offering of your body and mind to follow the Three Jewels of the Buddha, the Dharma, and the Sangha, which represent all buddhas, the authentic Dharma, and the holy Sangha. Thus, you cultivate according to the Buddhadharma and realize your inherent Buddha-nature.

In Vajrayana Buddhism, taking refuge with a vajra master is added to the Threefold Refuge, which then becomes the Fourfold Refuge. We thus recite the Fourfold Refuge Mantra: Namo Guru bei, Namo Buddha ye, Namo Dharma ye, Namo Sangha ye.

Vajrayana Buddhism places the vajra master [or guru] before the Buddha, the Dharma, and the Sangha so as to educate the Vajrayana practitioner that only the guru can transmit the Vajrayana doctrines, and the guru is indispensable when it comes to studying Vajrayana Buddhism. Hence the guru is the most important root of spirituality. The body of the guru symbolizes the Buddha himself being on earth. The speech of the guru symbolizes the Buddha expounding the Dharma. The mind of the guru symbolizes the original purity of the

Buddha. This is the reason why the vajra master is the embodiment of the Three Jewels of the Buddha, the Dharma, and the Sangha.

There is also the Sixfold Refuge in Vajrayana Buddhism. This is built upon the Fourfold Refuge and adds to it by taking refuge in the root personal deity and the root dharma protector. We know that the guru, the personal deity and the protector form the Three Roots [of Vajrayana Buddhism]. The guru is the root of blessings, the deity is the root of accomplishments, and the protector is the root of activities.

In principle, if one cultivates the Vajrayana teachings without the blessing and guidance of the heart essence and secret keys transmitted by the root guru, one will not know how to approach the system of Vajrayana practices. And without the mighty spiritual current of the root personal deity to empower the practitioner, how can he or she approach and enter into the secrets of all buddhas and attain spiritual resonance? Furthermore, without the constant protection offered to the Vajrayana practitioner by the root protector, he or she will be attacked and swallowed by the maras, or will end up crazy. Of these Three Roots, the guru ranks as the most important. This is because Vajrayana rules state that the practitioner must first receive the transmission of his personal deity and protector from his guru before he or she can cultivate those respective practices.

45. Blessing with Light

Once a photo was taken of me standing in front of many kneel-ing disciples. My raised hand formed a mudra, and a beam of light descended from the sky, radiating towards the disciples. The light was milky white and was glowing in sparkling brilliance.

This photo was captured coincidentally by a man with a camera at the moment I was giving blessings to my disciples. It was a photo that captured the "blessing with light."

In Vajrayana Buddhism, we often pray to our guru, personal de-ity and protector to offer us blessings at all times, and this naturally comes as the blessing with light.

Besides having our guru, personal deity and protector radiating light upon us, we must learn to visualize radiating light in our Vajray-ana practice.

For example, we recite the Great Compassion Dharani and visual-ize a moon disc on our heart where the white Sanskrit syllable HRIH sits. Visualize this syllable radiating light into a cup of water. Upon completion of our chanting, the cup of water shall become the "Great Compassion Dharani Water."

When we recite the Usnisa Vijaya Dharani, we need to visualize the white Sanskrit syllable KHAM imprinted in the moon disc within our hearts. The syllable KHAM radiates light that illuminates all sentient beings. Once touched by this light, a person's karma is removed, his body and mind refreshed, and he receives great wisdom.

When we recite the Mantra of Light, we must visualize a golden Sanskrit syllable AH seated in the moon disc within our hearts, radiating light to illuminate all sentient beings. Anyone who is touched by this light is removed from all suffering and receives joy.

It is the same for other mantra recitations. In Vajrayana Buddhism, such blessings with light are unimaginable. The light comes from empty space and enters into the heart of the practitioner. Through the seed syllable the light is radiated to deliver sentient beings. Through such actions, all beings dwelling in the six realms of samsara spanning all worlds shall swiftly receive great attainment.

Anyone who truly understands the workings of Vajrayana methods knows how precious these teachings are. The Vajrayana teachings can fulfill the wishes of all sentient beings in the six realms, and upon the blessing with light, all shall be liberated permanently from birth, old age, sickness, death, and all suffering.

Let me say this: the Blessing with Light is very real.

46. Invocation with Light

Somebody once asked me: "How do you invoke all the buddhas and deities in the Vajrayana teachings?"

I replied, "We must form the Invocation Mudra and chant the Invocation Mantra. First, the practitioner should hold the thought that all buddhas and bodhisattvas, the Three Jewels, are filling the space with their omnipresence. The assembly of buddhas and great bodhisattvas of the ten directions, seen with their majestic golden bodies, are seated on lotus thrones, encircling the field in endless multiple rows and radiating lights of great luminance."

"Are there any secret keys in the invocation?"

"Yes," I answered. For example, the secret key for invoking my personal deity, Amitabha Buddha, is called the "Invocation with Light." Visualize Amitabha Buddha's seed syllable HRIH seated within the moon disc at your heart chakra, radiating three beams of red light which travel upwards through the central channel, projecting through the crown chakra into space. At that time, Amitabha Buddha shall respond naturally with the light of invocation and descend.

Another secret key lies in the use of the Vajra Hook Mudra for invocation. The practitioner visualizes the hook attaching itself to the cloud that the respective buddha or bodhisattva rides upon, and the buddha or bodhisattva shall definitely descend.

Other approaches of invocation include:

Visualizing a lotus throne ascending to welcome and receive the respective buddha or bodhisattva.

Visualizing the respective buddha's or bodhisattva's sleeve fluttering as he or she approaches.

Visualizing the respective buddha or bodhisattva raising his or her foot.

Visualizing the jewels and adornments worn by the respective buddha or bodhisattva chiming as he or she moves.

In general, the most important of all invocation practices in Vajrayana Buddhism is the "Invocation with Light." The shining of the three lights relies completely on the workings of the heart. This means that your heart is radiating light of great luminosity. As long as your heart gives off light of great brilliance, countless buddhas and bodhisattvas shall all radiate light upon you.

The shining of light itself carries vast significance, which includes the significance of calling forth and invocation, the significance of seeking refuge, the significance of alertness, the significance of making offerings, the significance of merits, and the significance of infinite Dharma. In Vajrayana Buddhism, it carries the significance of infinite light!

If you use your heart and radiate light to invoke the buddhas and bodhisattvas, they shall definitely descend.

47. The Importance of the Four Preliminary Practices

I was asked, "What is the most important practice?"

"The Four Preliminary Practices," I replied.

"Why?"

"The Four Preliminary Practices are the very foundation of Vajrayana Buddhism. If the foundation is weak, all cultivation is simply like building castles in the air."

When we begin our cultivation of the Vajrayana practices, we must first build the foundation, as preparation for the ground of cultivation is needed, hence, we must do these preliminaries practices.

The Four Preliminary Practices are each embedded with profound significance. I shall elucidate on them:

1. The Fourfold Refuge.
2. The Great Homage.
3. The Great Mandala Offering.
4. The Vajrasattva Practice.

The Fourfold Refuge Practice is the recitation of the Fourfold Refuge Mantra to strengthen your spiritual conviction. The Great Homage functions to remove our karmic hindrances. The Great Mandala Offering is done to increase blessings and wisdom, and the Vajrasattva Practice is for the repentance of wrong actions.

To practice the Vajrayana teachings, one must gather a sufficient stock of blessings and wisdom. If both of these measures are insufficient, coupled with a lack of spiritual conviction, it will result in the growth of mara hindrances. Such an individual is not qualified to cultivate the Vajrayana practices.

A Vajrayana scripture states, "If one wishes to attain buddhahood without the accumulation of blessings and wisdom, it is like trying to extract oil by cooking sand."

Many have taken up the study of Vajrayana teachings for many years, and the more Vajrayana practices they learn, the more hindrances they face. In the end, they simply give up and leave. This is ridiculous. It simply reveals that the individuals have not built a firm foundation with the Four Preliminary Practices, and may not have had any spiritual resonance through them. Those who have attained spiritual resonance through the Four Preliminary Practices would never give up and leave.

Never look down upon the Four Preliminary Practices. It is of vital importance to strengthen our spiritual conviction, remove karmic hindrances, repent for our wrongdoings, and increase blessings and wisdom. Thus, we need to practice the Four Preliminary Practices earnestly, and practice them to perfection.

48. The Secret of Contemplating Emptiness

I have discovered a little secret which highlights the importance of contemplating emptiness before a Vajrayana practitioner begins his or her cultivation practice. As long as you still your thoughts and empty them, absorbed in this state for one split moment, the spiritual current from the Cosmic Consciousness shall empower you, flowing into your body and mind.

My personal experience on the procedure of this practice goes like this. I first visualize myself sitting on an eight-petalled lotus throne and a luminous moon disc appears before me. Following this, I recite the Contemplation of Emptiness Mantra (the Purification of Three Karmas Mantra):

[transliteration] Om, si-ba-wa, su-da, sa-er-wa, da-er-ma, si-ba-wa, su-do-hang (Recite 5 times)

[Sanskrit] OM SOBHAWA SHUDDHA SARWA DHARMA SOBHAWA SHUDDHO HAM.

Visualize the moon disc expanding until it is immeasurable massive.

I am merged with the pure moon disc.

Everything becomes emptiness.

At this moment of emptiness, the spiritual light current flows into my body and mind, filling my being, which at once responds with the eight sensations:

1. A tingling sensation - the body experiences a tingling sensation.
2. An itchy sensation - it feels like having insects crawling all over your body, resulting in an itchy feeling.
3. A light sensation - the body feels as light as a floating cloud.
4. A heavy sensation - the body feels heavy like an immovable mountain.
5. A cold sensation - the body feels as cold as water, yet as refreshing as ice.
6. A warm sensation - the body feels like it is on fire, yet it is comfortably warm.
7. A rigid sensation - the body feels stiff like a wooden board.
8. A slippery sensation - the body feels as slippery as grease.

This is why I say that when you cultivate one session of practice, it is as good as receiving an empowerment from the pure spiritual current of the universe. This is equivalent to having spiritual resonance with the spiritual current where you merge into it and kindle an exchange and interaction with the buddhas and bodhisattvas.

This Contemplation of Emptiness is the first secret of Yoga Tantra.

49. Elucidation on the Three Powers

There exist many Buddhist schools with a diversity of views and thoughts, separated by the way in which each responds to the karmic affinity and natural capacity of the cultivator.

My personal view on how I see Zen Buddhism, Pure Land Buddhism and Vajrayana Buddhism are as follows:

Zen Buddhism is established on a premise outside of words and beyond the doctrines of Buddhism. It directly reveals the mind and the attainment of buddhahood upon seeing Buddha-nature. It therefore encompassed the pure wisdom of enlightenment, as its body of essence is emptiness itself.

Pure Land Buddhism teaches that any person wants rebirth through nianfo [or nembutsu, reciting the Buddha name], can be reborn at any of the nine levels of lotus emanation. The individual, who responds to the dedication of Amitabha Buddha's power of great compassionate vows with great faith in his chanting, shall enter into the samadhi of the mindfulness of the Buddha [also samadhi of the recitation of the Buddha's name] and be delivered directly to the Western Paradise in the karmic body of a common mortal.

In the case of Vajrayana Buddhism, it relies on the vajra master to transmit the teachings, give blessings and empowerments. It also requires the establishment of a mandala, the recitation of mantras and the cultivation of practices, during which the practitioner forms mudras, practices visualization, and calls forth and invokes the personal deity to reveal its presence. Eventually, you are True Suchness, and you are Buddhadharma itself. It encompasses multiple levels of embedded profound secrets that are simply wonderful and mysterious.

In other words, Zen Buddhism relies on personal power.

The Pure Land School relies on external power.

Vajrayana Buddhism is a combination of personal power, external power and the guru's power.

Let me explain this. Zen Buddhism is the cultivation of thoughts, penetrating directly into the mind to reveal its very source so that one may attain buddhahood. It relies solely on personal effort to attain enlightenment.

Pure Land Buddhism relies on the deliverance from the Buddha, and thus it is all about external power. With recitation of the Buddha name and mindfulness of the Buddha, maintaining a constant flow of pure thoughts, and complete devotion to the chanting of the name of Amitabha Buddha, the heavy karma of eight billion kalpas of birth-and-death is eliminated. Hence, one is reborn in the buddhaland.

In Vajrayana Buddhism, it hinges on three powers. First is the blessing power of the root guru. When one achieves spiritual resonance with the personal deity, one receives the deity's power, which is external power. Finally, when the practitioner develops to the level that reveals his or her Buddha-nature, it is considered personal power. With the revelation of Buddha mind, one attains buddhahood in this very body. I feel that Zen Buddhism is the most difficult to practice, whereas Pure Land Buddhism is the easiest. Vajrayana Buddhism places great emphasis on the stages of cultivation, and holds the most profound of meanings.

50. Reverence for the *High King Avalokitesvara Sutra*

Someone asked, "Why is the recitation of the *High King Avalok-itesvara Sutra* [Gao Wang Jing] included in the sadhana of the True Buddha Tantra?"

I replied, "The *High King Avalokitesvara Sutra* is the assembly of the great names of all buddhas and bodhisattvas of the ten directions and three times. When we recite the *High King Avalokitesvara Sutra*, it is as good as prostrating before every buddha and bodhisattva."

Question: "How effective is the *High King Avalokitesvara Sutra*?"

My reply: "The sutra was widespread during China's Tang dynasty. Its effectiveness is magical and is definitely superior."

Question: "What are its advantages?"

My reply: "Seen from a transcendental viewpoint, it eliminates the suffering of samsara. Seen from a worldly viewpoint, it helps to remove all evil harm. When it comes to the repentance of past deeds, reciting the *High King Avalokitesvara Sutra* a thousand times shall eliminate all heavy karma, helping one to reach the Four Nirvana Virtues of eternity, bliss, true self and purity."

Question: "Can we include the *Heart Sutra* in the sadhana of the

True Buddha Tantra?"

My reply: "The *Heart Sutra* is the quintessence of the *Mahaprajna-paramita Sutra* and the *Diamond Sutra*, revealing the state of enlightenment. The Sutrayana and Vajrayana traditions place great importance in this scriptural text. It is all right to include the recitation of the *Heart Sutra* in your Vajrayana practice."

This is what I have to say: When I first had my divine eye opened by the Golden Mother of the Jade Pond at the Jade Emperor Temple in Taichung, the very first sutra I received at the temple was the *High King Avalokitesvara Sutra*. Thus, I revere the *High King Avalokitesvara Sutra*, as I feel it is our affinity.

Subsequently, when I recited the sutra, I realized the names of buddhas and bodhisattvas of the ten directions are summed up in this one sutra. Every time I recite the sutra, the lights of the Dharma Realm shine upon me. It is much like paying homage to the Three Jewels; much like receiving a great empowerment from the Dharma Realm; much like being purified by the spiritual light current of the Dharma Realm. It is simply incredible.

This is why I have included the *High King Avalokitesvara Sutra* in the practice of the True Buddha Tantra, and wish every True Buddha practitioner to benefit from it.

Of course, I understand that the true spiritual plane revealed through the *Heart Sutra* is supreme and unexcelled. It is the spiritual state of arriving at the other shore, which is deeply profound in its scope. The truth of Emptiness without form is simply awesome. I have memorized the sutra well. I have only the greatest respect for these two sutras.

The *High King Avalokitesvara Sutra* sums up the majestic names of the buddhas and bodhisattvas of the ten directions and three times, paying homage to the Three Jewels.

The *Heart Sutra* shows the arrival at the other shore, and calmly abiding in it.

51. A Buddha Manifestation of Great Authority

A monk from the Sutrayana tradition once asked me, "According to the Buddhist scriptures, the period between the time Shakyamuni Buddha entered Nirvana and the time of the appearance of Maitreya Buddha is known as the Buddha-less World. This means a period of time where no Buddha is found living on earth. Do you agree with this viewpoint?"

I asked the monk, "Why do you practice Buddhism?"

The monk answered, "To become a Buddha."

I said, "Since there can be no attainment of buddhahood, why do you want to study Buddhism?" The monk was speechless.

From what I know, after Shakyamuni Buddha entered Nirvana, many have attained buddhahood in their very bodies; for example, Padmasambhava, who was the second Buddha of Uddiyana, Milarepa, Tsongkhapa, and so on. Manjushri Bodhisattva was enlightened in the North, whose title is "the Treasury of Utmost Joy Mani Gem Buddha." Sariputra, one of the main disciples of the Buddha, was given the title "Lotus Light Buddha." The five hundred Arhats, on attaining buddhahood, will be collectively known as "Samantaprabhasa, the Pervading Light Buddha." In the *Lotus Sutra*, it says, "The daughter of the dragon king Sagara who had turned eight, conceived the desire for bodhi in the space of an instant, and attained Supreme Perfect Enlightenment in the Spotless World of the South." This was how a dragon girl became a Buddha.

I told the monk, "These are all examples of attaining buddhahood. Many people in Zen Buddhism have attained buddhahood as well, for they have gained realization through seeing their true nature." The *Platform Sutra of the Sixth Patriarch* says, "If you discern your own original mind and see your own original nature, you are what they call a great man, a teacher of devas and men, a Buddha."

The monk, fumbling away, uttered, "But why does the scripture state it that way?"

I replied, "Shakyamuni Buddha would never forbid any sentient beings to attain buddhahood during this period, neither would he stop anyone from attaining buddhahood in this very body. The scripture was misinterpreted by later generations of Buddhist students. From what I know, the appearance of Shakyamuni Buddha in the Saha world marks the appearance of a Buddha of great authority. And likewise, it will be the same for Maitreya Buddha when he delivers sentient beings during the time of the Nagapuspa Assembly. The time between these two events is filled with many cases of beings attaining buddhahood."

In Zen Buddhism, you can see your True Nature and attain enlightenment. In Vajrayana Buddhism, you can gain the perfect attainment of the Truth body, the Bliss body and the Emanation body, and realize the Supreme Bodhi, becoming a Buddha in this very lifetime. The *Essentials of Vajrayana* says, "While the doctrines of Vajrayana may differ in their scope of approach, they all aim to use the physical body given by your parents to attain buddhahood in this very body within your lifetime."

52. Merging as One

The quintessence of Vajrayana lies in yoga, and yoga means "union" [or spiritual resonance]. Of course, this "union" is a very secret matter. Thus, it is said in the book, The *Essentials of Vajrayana*, "The meaning of the word secret is secret mystery, or profound secret, seen within the context of a hidden mystery. It is a realm concealed in deep secrecy, which is the doctrine of cultivation born of self realized wisdom."

It is my understanding that with spiritual resonance, there is the function of the "blessing of miraculous transformation." With this blessing of miraculous transformation comes the three inconceivable bodies:

the Dharmakaya - the body of self nature
the Sambhogakaya - the body of enjoyment
the Nirmanakaya - the body of blessings

Regarding Yoga Tantra, Venerable Master Yinguang once said, "The Three Secrets of Vajrayana produce the blessing of miraculous transformation, which helps the common mortal attain fruition in this lifetime. Its merits and activities are beyond thoughts and descriptive words. Hence, it is known as the unimaginable force."

Thus, the *Mahavairocana Sutra* says, "The profound Dharma that has no form cannot be understood by those with inferior wisdom. In order to reach the beings of inferior capacity, the Dharma of form is delivered simultaneously."

The key to this Dharma of form is the visualization of the merging of self and deity [Ruwo-Woru]. One visualizes:

1. The pure moon disc.
2. The emergence of a Sanskrit seed syllable.
3. The emergence of the personal deity.
4. The personal deity abiding above the center of the crown. The deity shrinks and enters the central channel and descends to the heart of the practitioner, and sits on the lotus of the heart. Then the deity expands to the size of the practitioner.
5. The practitioner and the deity are indivisible and indistinguishable and in one instant, the practitioner becomes the deity and the deity becomes the practitioner.

I am telling you in all honesty that when you form the mudra, recite the mantra and engage in the Ruwo-Woru visualization, you are at an equal level with the Three Secrets [of body, speech, and mind] of the Tathagata, and thus possess limitless meritorious functions. This is the truth of spiritual resonance.

Once the practitioner achieves spiritual resonance and becomes one with the personal deity, he or she gains access to the Dharma Realm through this single gateway.

In all honesty and sincerity, I must state that this is absolutely true.

53. The Key Instructions of Entering, Abiding and Absorbing

The cultivation practice of Vajrayana Buddhism is basically divided into two parts. The first part involves the cultivation practice of the spiritual resonance of the Three Secrets. The second part involves the cultivation practice of vital winds, channels and drops.

From what I know, the cultivation of these two parts shares the key instruction of "entering, abiding and absorbing." This key is of vital importance to your cultivation.

In the part that involves the spiritual resonance of the Three Secrets, the practitioner invites the personal deity to "enter" into his or her body and "abide" in it. Following which, the personal deity and the practitioner are mutually "absorbed" into each other. When the absorption is reached, countless numbers of bodhisattvas from the ten directions, as well as all protectors, will instantly gather and encircle the practitioner. Ornamented with adamantine adornments, lights of great brilliance are emitted from the practitioner's heart, and infinite streams of light rays are emitted from every pore, illuminating the worlds of the ten directions.

As long as the practitioner gains purification of his body, speech, and mind, achieves response with the Three Secrets, and cultivates properly according to the instructions to "enter, abide and absorb," he shall realize innate wisdom and enter the primordial ground. In joy, he proceeds gradually in stages, until he finally attains the unhindered Dharmakaya of the Tathagata.

The second part involves the cultivation of vital winds, channels and drops:

The practitioner inhales a breath of air (wind) and let it enter into the dan-tian [lower abdomen] area.

This breath of air should constantly abide in the dan-tian.

This breath of air is absorbed into all the meridians and channels and reaches every pore.

(This is the secret key in which the breath of air or wind enters, abides, and becomes absorbed in the body.)

When the air enters, it must go right into the dan-tian. Where the breath is concerned, the longer you can hold it, the better. To my knowledge, the longer this breath of air abides, the more likely it will find its way into the central channel. The final secret key is to "inhale first, then release," which means when you can no longer hold your breath, instead of releasing, inhale another breath of air which presses downwards, forcing all the vital winds into the central channel. Then direct the breath of air or wind throughout all meridians and channels, and let it be absorbed into every pore.

Upon comparing the first and second part of the cultivation, you can imagine how important it is to work on "entering, abiding and absorbing." Now you know why Padmasambhava said, "All the merits of Vajrayana arise from the practice of Vase Breathing."

54. Seen in the Context of Heresy

Vajrayana Buddhism often finds itself the target of criticism, accused of being heretical. Naturally there are many reasons contributing to this, but most accusations are founded on a lack of understanding of the Vajrayana doctrines, as well as on false allegations.

For example, some have painted Vajrayana Buddhism as Brahmanism, as they feel that Vajrayana Buddhism's wide inclusion of every spectrum of celestial beings is similar to Brahmanism. The truth is that Vajrayana Buddhism is no different from Mahayana Buddhism when it comes to delivering sentient beings out of the ocean of suffering, away from the three lower realms.

Some have made the remark that Vajrayana Buddhism promotes spiritual powers and uses the power of gods to perform divination, check the records of past lives, pray for rain, give healing, use chart astrology and perform geomancy. These phenomena are similar in nature to the activities of ghosts and the occult, and based on this assumption, they call Vajrayana a heresy.

Fundamentally speaking, the talk on Vajrayana Buddhism being associated with divination, astrology, geomancy, praying for rain and healing barely scratches the surface of the miscellaneous aspects of Vajrayana Buddhism. The true Vajrayana teachings involve the doctrines of vajra disciplinary rules, the bodhi mind, liberation from samsara, and attaining buddhahood in this very body. Therefore Vajrayana Buddhism cuts away all illusions and realizes what is true and real. It is very different from the way that some pseudo masters are practicing - by amassing wealth and by womanizing.

Some have said that the homa rituals conducted in Vajrayana Buddhism are similar to the fire offering rituals of Zoroastrianism from Persia. Thus, Buddhists should stop conducting homas. To my knowledge, a Vajrayana homa involves the use of mudra, and therefore will achieve results. It utilizes a shrine to work its powers, moving the forces with the mind. The homa practice anchors on the mind itself. This is why Tsongkhapa considered the homa to be one of the three accomplishments.

Then there are remarks about the Completion Stage of the Inner Tantra being the cultivation of vital winds, channels and drops. They say that the Completion Stage focuses only on the building of physical health, which is the cultivation of the physical body. This deviates from the path of mind training, so thus it is a heresy. I want to clarify that the Vajrayana practice of qi or vital winds advocates the blending of mind and qi - that mind is qi, and qi cannot exist without the mind. Through the training of qi or vital winds, we can validate the mind. There is no separation from the mind. And eventually, through the practice of vital winds, channels and drops, we can validate the presence of the Secret Adorned Mind [or "the mind of secret sublimity"; Japanese: Himitsu-shogon-Shin]. This is the spiritual ground of Vajrayana. Therefore, how could anyone accuse Vajrayana teachings of deviating from the mind?

I feel that it is our great privilege and blessing to find the Vajrayana teachings, offered to us as a rare and special affinity. We must never slander its doctrines!

55. The Importance of Cultivating Qi or Vital Winds

A Chinese physician told me that he had treated a senior monk for his illness. When he checked the monk's pulse, he was shocked to discover that the monk's body of meridians and channels showed signs of blockage. In fact all of his channels had been damaged, forming strains of Yin or dysfunctional channels.

The Chinese physician also mentioned a senior nun who had been ill since childhood. The circulation of qi and blood in her body was gravely disrupted. She was constantly suffering from the torment of her illness, which was sad to see. If she could not save herself, how could she deliver sentient beings?

The physician asked the senior monk, "With your health, how can you cultivate?"

The monk replied, "We cultivate the mind, not the body."

"But isn't it equally important to strengthen our health and cultivate qi?" the physician remarked. "That's heresy!" the senior monk refuted.

I personally disagree with the views of the senior monk. Think about the Zen Patriarch Bodhidharma, who sailed north from India and became the first Chinese Zen Patriarch. His teaching of the Dharma is by way of mind transmission, and the essence of mind was transmitted secretly between patriarchs. However, when Bodhidharma observed that the health of the Shaolin monks had deteriorated from prolonged sitting meditation, he feared that they might go astray in their meditation. Hence, he decided to teach them the martial arts and also the Yijinjing [also known as "The Muscle-Tendon Change Classic," which is a qi and body strengthening program].

Bodhidharma believes in treating sentient beings' afflictions with the appropriate antidotes. Whether it was striking students with a staff or shouting at them [to clear mental obscurations] or teaching physical exercises to promote the unobstructed flow of qi and blood, he was flexible in applying the essence of the teachings, according to the circumstances and capacity of the students. Bodhidharma actually said that a practitioner who only cultivated the mind and not the body was likely to go astray. Thus, we have the heritage of Shaolin kungfu handed down since that time.

Vajrayana Buddhism places equal emphasis on the parallel cultivation of mind and body. Our health forms the very basis of our cultivation.

Vajrayana Buddhism also clearly states: "To cultivate qi is equivalent to harmonizing the mind. When the mind is harmonized, our qi is calm and smooth."

When a person who cultivates qi experiences a smooth circulation of his qi and blood, and finds comfort in his body, his mind shall naturally be at ease and eventually, his defilement is uprooted.

The Vajrayana teachings include the Vajra Fist Exercises to help regulate the qi.

I advocate that it is vital to cultivate qi if one wishes to blend the mind with qi.

56. Cultivation through the Use of the Four Elements

Vajrayana Buddhism views everything, including mountains, rivers and the earth, as matrixes formed from the four elements of earth, water, fire and wind. And this world is known as the material world.

Humans are part of the material world, as the human body is a structure formed by the four elements of earth, water, fire and wind. To my knowledge, the cultivation practices of Vajrayana make use of the individual nature of these four elements to conceive the true nature of Prajnaparamita, Supreme Perfect Enlightenment, the Vairocana Great Ocean of Light, and attain the innate wisdom of the Tathagata.

I shall elucidate on how the four elements are applied to cultivate the vital winds, channels and drops:

1. Earth - Channels
2. Water - Drops
3. Fire - Inner fire
4. Wind - Qi or vital winds

The practice of cultivating vital winds, channels and drops is based on the very principle and fundamental essence that once the practitioner has reached a certain level with his or her cultivation of vital winds or qi, he or she may enter into the Vajravarahi Inner Fire Meditation, igniting the inner fire with his or her breath of qi. When the inner fire rises through the central channel, reaches the top of the crown and touches the thousand-petalled lotus, the white drop begins to drip, resulting in "blazing and dripping."

"Blazing and dripping" is the situation where water is above fire, and as water drips downwards and the fire rises, clear light is produced. It also clears the five chakras along the central channel, as well as opening the rest of the meridians and minor channels.

When the central channel is cleared and the heart chakra is opened, the light of the heart shall naturally illuminate. All discursive thoughts naturally subside, and your nature is constantly pure. With afflictions removed, what is visible will be the clear and bright Buddha-nature and the Buddha Pure Land. The individual shall instantly attain buddhahood in this very body.

I have divided the practice of vital winds, channels and drops into the sub-categories of Vase Breathing, inner fire practice, the practice of drops, the non-leakage practice, the opening of the central channel, the opening of the five chakras, and so on. Every one of these practices must be accomplished accordingly in stages, for there are many pith instructions to these practices that require oral transmission from the guru. Otherwise, one should never attempt to practice them blindly.

Upon accomplishment of this practice, the attainment of siddhi is a certainty. The guru holds the pith instructions that are reliable and proven.

57. The Body Mandala

Once, I went mountain climbing with many of my disciples. Several of them had come from Europe, and their flight was scheduled for departure that very afternoon. When two of my disciples learned that their personal deity was the Medicine Buddha, they immediately knelt down on the spot, gave their offerings and requested the personal deity empowerment.

At that time, I was dressed only in a lama robe, without the necessary ritual vase [bumpa], the Buddha crown and the Dharma throne. Needless to say, there was no mandala available for this purpose. I thought about this and agreed to their request. I said, "All right. I'll give both of you the personal deity empowerment. I want you to form the Medicine Buddha mudra and recite the Medicine Buddha mantra, and visualize the Medicine Buddha seated on top of your crown."

I extended my hand to touch their crowns, and gave them the empowerment. Then I explained to my disciples: All Vajrayana empowerments should ideally take place in the sanctuary of a mandala [or shrine], because the shrine houses the combined merits of all buddhas and deities. When the vajra master wears the Buddha crown and ascends the Dharma throne, he gives the respective empowerment either with the image of the deity or the ritual vase. This symbolizes an empowerment given to the disciple with the power of the personal deity, the power of the guru and the power of the Dharma Realm. Only then can an empowerment be considered valid.

Otherwise, it is not permissible and not in accordance with the Dharma to offer the empowerment in wild mountainous areas. Without his Buddha crown, without the Dharma throne to which the guru ascends, without ritual objects and the mandala, the entire empowerment is considered invalid.

In that case, how come I could give the empowerment? I have already achieved spiritual resonance with the Five Buddhas. In an instant, the Five Buddhas arrived on the top of my head and transformed themselves into a precious crown. The ground that I stood on was instantly transformed into the lotus throne. My hands were my ritual objects and abiding within my five chakras - namely the third eye chakra, the throat chakra, the heart chakra, the navel chakra [also called the manipura chakra], and the sacral chakra [also called the svadhisthana chakra] - were the Five Buddhas and Five Herukas. Hence, you shall find the assembly of sages residing within my body, where a multitude of meritorious virtues converge. My body itself is the mandala.

I wish to inform the True Buddha practitioner that by the cultivation of vital winds, channels and drops, one can develop the Body Mandala.

1. Vital winds or qi - Functions in all accomplishments.
2. Channels - Transformed into every realm, and the Buddha Pure Land.
3. Drops - Buddhahood.
4. Inner fire - Clear light.

If your cultivation and attainment in your practice of vital winds, channels and drops reach a stage where a transformation occurs, you will realize Thusness or True Reality. True Reality is without individual nature, and adjusts to changes without holding to a fixed self-nature. Impurity and purity, truth and delusion intertwine with no hindrances in an infinite matrix of interaction.

Vajrayana Buddhism places the utmost importance in the sadhana. If the sadhana is incomplete, then all is considered invalid!

Yet, only by cultivating and attaining the Body Mandala can one rise above and beyond all things! Only then can one hold the key to infinite Buddhadharma without fail!

Who can validate this statement: "I am the True Reality?"

My reply: "One who practices vital winds, channels and drops."

The Vajrayana practitioner must understand the five vital winds, namely the ascending wind, equalizing wind, descending wind, pervading wind, and life-essence wind.

Sheng-yen Lu

58. The Key Instructions to Cultivating Vital Winds

Sit either in the crossed-legged vajra position [the full lotus position] or the half lotus position, with the dignified demeanor of a Buddha. With your hands forming Amitabha Buddha's Dhyana Mudra, you hold your spine erect, shoulders straight, slightly tilting your neck while holding the chin inwards against the throat. Your tongue presses against the upper palate, and your eyes look to the ground about two feet in front of you. When you sit in this way, your body and mind settle down and maintains its stability.

Inhale a breath of air down to the dan-tian [in the lower abdomen], pushing down the ascending vital winds and drawing up the descending vital winds, where [with muscular control] the vital winds are cupped in a vase. Hold your breath for as long as you can, until you can no longer retain the vital winds. A vital pith instruction at this point is to inhale another breath of air which forces the remaining vital winds into the central channel, reaching the heart center and dissolving into the other chakras, eventually traveling to every pore and is then released through them.

The unabsorbed vital winds or qi is exhaled through the nostrils, shooting up like an arrow. The pith instructions to cultivating vital winds are as follows:

The spine must remain straight and erect - only then can the central channel remain straight.

The chin pressing slightly down and inward - the ascending wind shall be forced downwards.

Tighten the pelvic muscles - the descending wind will be drawn upwards.

The tongue presses against the upper palate - only then can the central channel be linked to the crown chakra.

Pressing the ascending wind downwards and drawing the descending wind upwards - only then can the vital winds or qi enter the central channel.

The practice of Vase Breathing aims to direct vital winds or qi into the central channel. As soon as the vital winds enter the central channel, a reaction occurs. The vital winds that enter into the central channel are referred to as the wisdom wind.

When you practice the Vase Breathing meditation long enough, all meridians and channels in your body shall remain clear and open, with a smooth circulation of qi, and your qi will be sufficient. This is known in the Taoist teachings as the Macrocosmic and Microcosmic Circulations.

The Vajrayana practitioner must understand the five vital winds, namely the ascending wind, equalizing wind, descending wind, pervading wind, and life-essence wind. From the action of vital winds, one ignites the inner fire, through which the clear and pure drops are formed. When the non-leakage drops are developed, one attains great bliss, clear light and emptiness.

59. Leakage Leads to a Spiritual Downfall

The word leakage was originally another term for afflictions, which carries the meaning of leakage or dissipation. When we are troubled and worried at all times, the primal qi or essence within us continuously leaks through the six sense organs, and this leakage leads to a spiritual downfall. This spiritual downfall implies falling into the three lower realms.

To my knowledge, the areas of "leakage" include the leakage of speech, leakage of body, and leakage of mind. The leakage of speech includes lying, slander, abusive speech, and lewd or bawdy language. The leakage of body includes killing, stealing, debauchery, and drinking alcohol. The leakage of mind includes greed, anger, and ignorance. I read the *Golden Mother of the Jade Pond on Liberation Sutra* and the Golden Mother says, "Death comes with leakage, and it is through the same areas where the vital and spiritual energies of humans have dissipated that they have to be replenished." This shows that leakage does refer to a body contaminated with afflictions.

The human body is indeed a vessel of leakage. For example, a woman experiences leakage through menstruation, and a man through the discharge of semen. In Vajrayana Buddhism, the discharge of menstrual fluid from the female is known as "red bodhicitta." The male's semen is called the drop or "white bodhicitta."

Among the cultivation practices of Vajrayana Buddhism is the non-leakage practice, which conditions the male practitioner to attain permanent non-leakage of semen, and the female practitioner to attain permanent non-leakage of menstrual fluid. Thus, the non-leakage practice helps the Vajrayana practitioner develop the non-leakage vajra body, which is indestructible.

My view is that leakage can be divided into a visible form of leakage and an invisible form of leakage. Invisible leakage comprises of the afflictions of greed, anger, and ignorance. Visible leakage is the discharge of menstrual fluid and semen. Whether the leakage is of the visible or invisible kind, it would still affect the cultivator.

A true practitioner should be pure of heart and be free of desires, cutting off all afflictions in the spiritual aspect of cultivation. And in the physical aspect of cultivation, he or she can cultivate the non-leakage practice and completely prevent the leakage of semen or menstrual blood. Only then can one achieve true liberation of body and mind, and achieve fearlessness.

Only upon the liberation of body and mind, being free from all delusions and contamination, can it be called "non-leakage."

60. An Introduction to the Contemplation of the Non-Leakage Practice

The visualization and cultivation of the non-leakage practice is classified as a special practice in Vajrayana Buddhism. It is viewed as one of the highest secrets, and is only transmitted to those with the proper empowerment. Thus, I shall only offer a simple introduction to this practice.

The foundation of this practice is Vase Breathing. In the training of Vase Breathing, you must achieve full breathing capacity. When qi or wind is directed into the central channel, the qi shoots up to the crown chakra. Only then can you cultivate the non-leakage practice.

There are three pith instructions to this practice:

1. The mantra - HUM.
2. The mudra - Form the Grip Mudra, by first folding the thumb inwards, and gripping it with the four fingers. Do this with both hands.
3. The visualization.

The method of visualization is as follows:

First, visualize the syllable HUM at the navel chakra. The tail of the syllable HUM extends out of the root chakra and hooks onto a white lotus flower (for a male practitioner) or a red lotus flower (for a female practitioner). The practitioner, while forming the Grip Mudra, lowers his hands.

The practitioner practices one round of Vase Breathing, shouts HUM, and lifts both hands upwards while keeping the Grip Mudra. At this point, the qi rushes towards the crown, and the seed syllable HUM pulls the lotus flower upwards along the central channel. The root chakra (referring to the male genitals) curls and follows into the central channel and reaches the crown chakra.

At the crown chakra is positioned, in order of appearance: the syllable HUM, followed by the lotus flower, and finally the usnisa (or protuberance) on the male practitioner's head. This protuberance is absent in female practitioners. What I wish to elucidate is: The white lotus flower is the semen, while the red lotus flower is the menstrual blood. The root chakra is the male genitals that [in the visualization] rises to the crown chakra and forms the protuberance. The female practitioner naturally does not have this protuberance.

The vital key to this practice is the single breath of Vase Breathing. The qi shoots up to the crown chakra, carrying with it the semen or menstrual energy to the head. In Vajrayana Buddhism this is called "raising the drops and leaping over Mount Sumeru." When you can elevate the drops, you can attain non-leakage.

The non-leakage practice must be supplemented by the three movements of Vajra Fist Exercises, which help to contain the semen and menstrual fluid and prevent them from discharging.

To my knowledge, as long as the practitioner is willing to cultivate this non-leakage practice diligently, keeping a daily practice schedule in the early morning, he or she should see results in half a year, or in three years at the latest.

When you attain accomplishment in this practice, containing ev-

129

ery bit of drop in the body, you shall feel very energized in your health and spirit. With this vitality, your cultivation of other practices shall achieve maximum result with much less effort.

Note: The pith instructions of the non-leakage practice must be transmitted orally in detail by a [genuine] vajra master.

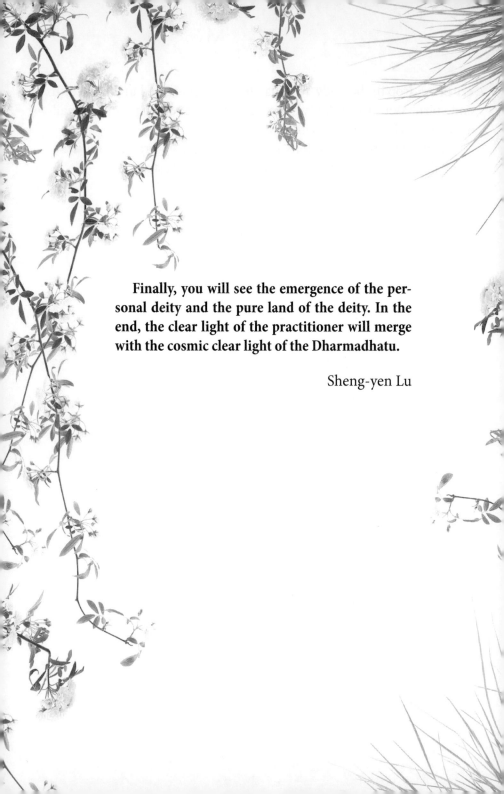

Finally, you will see the emergence of the personal deity and the pure land of the deity. In the end, the clear light of the practitioner will merge with the cosmic clear light of the Dharmadhatu.

Sheng-yen Lu

61. A Look at Validation

A disciple asked, "When we purify our body, speech and mind, what do we hope to validate?" My reply was, "The Yoga of One Taste."

The disciple asked again, "When we cultivate the vital winds, channels and drops, what can we hope to validate?"

I replied, "The appearance of clear light."

I have said that the union of the Three Secrets refers to the Three Secrets of the body, speech and mind of the practitioner being merged indivisibly with the Three Secrets of the body, speech and mind of the personal deity. This is known as the Yoga of One Taste. At this stage, the physical body born of your parents is the same as that of the personal deity.

Practitioners who achieve results with the Three Secrets shall find that when they cultivate the karma yogas of purification, enhancement, harmonization, and subjugation, they can eradicate transgressions and calamities, contain epidemics, heal illnesses, increase blessings and wisdom, enhance relationships and defeat all enemies. Such achievements will result in incredible merits.

Let me say that in the cultivation of vital winds, channels, and drops through the Inner Fire Yoga, you will first see the appearance of a drop of clear light, followed by the light of a vajra chain. Finally, you will see the emergence of the personal deity and the pure land of the deity. In the end, the clear light of the practitioner will merge with the cosmic clear light of the Dharmadhatu.

If you accomplish the Inner Fire Yoga when cultivating vital winds, channels and drops, you may proceed to cultivate Dream Yoga, Illusory Body Yoga, Clear Light Yoga, Phowa Yoga or Consciousness Transference Yoga. These [and the Bardo Yoga] constitute the Six Yogas of Naropa.

Heruka Practice helps you accomplish all activities.

The Highest Yoga Tantra helps the practitioner attain purity.

The Great Perfection allows you to attain complete freedom.

In my twenty years of spreading the Dharma and giving talks, I have gone to great lengths to explain these practices in detail, revealing what is necessary and even revealing some details that should not be revealed. What remains are the supremely secret teachings and techniques that I shall only reveal in person to the right candidates with the affinity and spiritual capacity.

My validation is:

The Dharma that is free from falsehood is defined as Right. The wisdom that is without boundary is defined as All Pervasive. Leaving the dream of samsara is defined as Awareness.

62. The Phenomena and Signs of Attaining Spiritual Resonance

Someone asked, "When Vajrayana practitioners attain spiritual resonance from mantra chanting and cultivation, what are the phenomenon and signs that will occur?"

My reply was, "As Vajrayana practitioners, when you recite mantras and cultivate your practices diligently, you will experience many phenomena and signs of spiritual resonance. These phenomena are seen during meditation, in the dream state or even the waking state. For example, you may see the appearance of buddhas, bodhisattvas or your personal deity. You may find yourself flying through space in total freedom, or you may reach any of the buddha pure lands. These are signs of great validation.

"You may also see lotus thrones, may experience consuming white fruits and vomiting dark filth, or swallowing the sun, the moon and the stars. You may see yourself radiating light, or may find yourself combing your hair where many worms will drop away. Such are the signs of karmic clearance.

"An individual who could not comprehend a sutra previously will now understand it with clarity, memorize it, and be able to, from its scriptural text, weave a multitude of insights. Your wisdom shall improve, and you shall gain mastery in all sutras, vinayas and sastras. If you think of your personal deity, you shall at once become one with the deity. You are approaching the level of accomplishment, which is the Yoga of One Taste.

"Some may see different lights, while others would see a variety of strange blossoms of lotus flowers. Some may see smoke, fire or light, or may find buddha statues or canopies moving. Some may hear celestial music being played, or experience the growth of a new tooth, or find that their white hair is turning black again. These are signs of the eradication of greed, anger and ignorance."

My view is that when Vajrayana practitioners gain spiritual resonance, they should neither reject nor grasp them, and should not be overjoyed, but rather should look at them as normal. They must continue their practice diligently, and should not become vain and proud. However, they may share these experiences with their fellow practitioners and seniors as a way of mutual encouragement, but not for self-glorification and personal benefits.

When practitioners attain spiritual resonance in samadhi, they experience an enhancement of blessings and wisdom, and yet know that all that they encounter is dream-like and illusory, for they realize the truth that the Dharma Realm exists as a singular non-dualistic reality.

At this point, you come to know that you are abiding in an immovable state of absolute being, where you can freely express yourself and exercise your spiritual powers and attain Supreme Perfect Enlightenment. At this point, you seek only buddhahood.

63. The Nine Levels of Accomplishment of the True Buddha Tantra

Question: "When a practitioner cultivates the True Buddha Tantra and achieves spiritual resonance, what is the attainment?"

My answer, "You can classify this into nine levels of accomplishment."

I shall explain these levels starting from the initial level to the highest level as follows:

The first level of attainment: anything you wish for shall be granted. Your wishes are accomplished by the dharma protectors. The eight divisions of spiritual beings - the devas, nagas, yaksas, gandharvas, asuras, garudas, kinnaras and mahoragas - shall respect you. You can exorcize evil spirits, bind ghosts, and perform healings.

The second level of attainment: you can command ghosts and celestial beings. You can summon celestial beings to descend and you can gain access to the treasury of sutras kept in the celestial or earthly realms and read them. You can enter the palaces of dragons, along with the palaces of the mountain gods.

The third level of attainment: you have full knowledge of your past lives. You know your past lives and those of others. You have attained the attainment of an earth immortal. You can travel freely in space and ascend to the celestial realms. You have attained the way of the immortal.

The fourth level of attainment: an illuminated immortal lord. You hold the status of a heavenly lord in the celestial realms, and your merits and wisdom are unsurpassed in the Trailokya or the Three Realms. You are also accomplished in spiritual travel.

The fifth level of attainment: a chakravarti (universal monarch). You have attained the five supernatural powers and your life span is infinite. However, you still live in the imperfect finite world of creation and enjoy great freedom. Your features are simply flawless.

The sixth level of attainment: the attainment of the first through fourth bodhisattva stages of fruition.

The seventh level of attainment: the attainment of the fifth through seventh bodhisattva stages of fruition.

The eighth level of attainment: the attainment of the eighth bodhisattva stage and above.

The ninth level of attainment: the attainment of Supreme Perfect Enlightenment, teacher of gods and men, in other words, a Buddha.

(The ten stages of the development of a bodhisattva are: 1. Pramudita [joy]; 2. Vimala [purity]; 3. Prabhakari [luminous]; 4. Arcismati [flaming wisdom]; 5. Sudurjaya [overcome difficulty]; 6. Abhimukhi [open way]; 7. Duramgama [far reaching]; 8. Acala [unperturbed]; 9. Sadhumati [discriminatory wisdom]; 10. Dharma megha [law cloud].)

Let me say this. These nine stages of attainment, attained through the cultivation of the True Buddha Tantra, are only a broad and general classification, for these spiritual realms of realization are simply inconceivable in the first place. There are individuals who have already attained the divine eye upon reaching the second level and others who have attained the Buddha Eye upon attaining the seventh level, so it is hard to say for certain what could happen. Therefore this classification can only serve as a broad reference.

Hence, the practitioner should begin with one mantra, one practice and one personal deity, and cultivate earnestly.

Sheng-yen Lu

64. One Mantra, One Practice, and One Personal Deity

A disciple asked me, "Is it better to recite many mantras or just stick to one?"

I replied, "It's all the same. All the same."

Expanding from this question, we may ask if it is better to cultivate just one practice or to cultivate multiple practices. Is it better to stick to one personal deity or to work with many?

My master once instructed me on this. Regarding this matter, it really depends on the individual's wishes. Some Vajrayana practitioners like to embrace the idea of multiple mantras, multiple practices and multiple personal deities. If the practitioner has sufficient time to apply to his cultivation and he is an ordained monk whose focus is on his cultivation, he can certainly practice this way. Therefore, as long as you have sufficient time to devote to practices, you can cultivate three, five, ten or even a hundred practices, a hundred deities, and it is all right.

However, most modern people are busy at work and spend little time at home. And when it comes to Vajrayana practice, it is almost impossible to cope with the cultivation of multiple mantras, multiple practices and multiple personal deities. Therefore, one can only carry out the cultivation of a single mantra, a single practice, and a single personal deity. Note that by focusing on one mantra, one practice and one deity, the very action of focusing opens the gateway to swift accomplishment, as it is easier to achieve spiritual resonance this way. Thus:

> The cultivation of multiple mantras, multiple practices and multiple deities offers the advantage of a wide network of affinity.
>
> The cultivation of one mantra, one practice and one deity promises swift spiritual resonance.

I often say that after you gain spiritual resonance with one personal deity, it will be easier to achieve spiritual resonance with other deities. It goes to say that when you gain spiritual resonance with one practice, you shall have success with every practice, accomplishing all that produces good merits. Hence, the practitioner should begin with one mantra, one practice and one personal deity, and cultivate earnestly. In the beginning stage, it is advisable not to dabble in too many things.

As True Buddha practitioners, we must remember that we need to complete the required amount of recitations of the guru mantra, the mantra of the personal deity and the mantra of the protector. When you achieve spiritual resonance with Guru Yoga, you are not far from achieving spiritual resonance through the Personal Deity Yoga and the Protector Practice.

This is because when you achieve spiritual resonance with your guru, the personal deity and protectors will naturally come along and descend to bless you with joy!

65. Ways of Reciting Mantras

Someone asked me, "It is known that there are many ways of reciting mantras, so which way is the best?"
I replied, "Indeed there are many ways to recite mantras, and it depends on the individual's affinity to find the best way for his or her to chant. Each person has his or her own habits and preferences, and therefore the merits of reciting mantras are expressed in wondrous ways."
I shall list the different ways of reciting mantras as follows:

1. Loud and audible recitation - the merit of this approach is that all who hear the mantra shall have their karmic transgression removed. When reciting aloud, you may choose to use the mala or prayer beads for counting, or simply chant without the mala.

2. Soft recitation - it is audible to your ears. Recite at an easy and comfortable pace, ensuring that each syllable is recited clearly. This approach helps you calm the mind.

3. The Vajra recitation - the lips remain sealed and the tongue should not touch the palate, moving slightly within

the mouth. This method of recitation is used in a crowded place. When traveling overseas, riding on boats, cars, or planes, you can use this method.

4. Breathing recitation - while breathing, imagine the Sanskrit mantra syllables flowing with the breath; an inflow of syllables with each inhalation of breath, and an outflow of syllables with each exhaling breath. Every mantra syllable is recited clearly, weaving the mantra syllables like a continuous string of luminous pearls that goes on and on. This is an approach that combines the breath counting visualization method with mantra recitation. Its merits are remarkable, and the way of visualization is wonderful.

5. Yogic recitation - visualize the moon disc in your heart chakra in all its pure clarity. Within the moon disc is imprinted a Sanskrit seed syllable, surrounded by the Sanskrit mantra syllables. Visualize the mantra syllables moving clockwise in a full circle. This is the yogic recitation. If the practitioner enters samadhi through this recitation method, he shall become one with his personal deity, the merits of which are simply endless.

Mantra recitation also includes the process of empowering the mala seven times with a mantra, which has a multiplying effect of a thousand times for every complete round of recitation. This is the Thousand Wheel Turning Technique, which I have transmitted before. This approach to mantra recitation increases merits swiftly.

66. Mantras are a Dharma Ship

Many who recite mantras wish to know the meaning behind the mantras. I am often approached with this question. My reply is: "Mantras are embedded with a wide range of meanings and significance, and any translation would not do them justice. Therefore they are not given any translation."

The *Commentary of the Nirvana Sutra* states, "Mantras are the secret language that flow out from the hearts of Buddhas. It is not translated because the translator is unable to comprehend it."

The *Commentary on the Wisdom of Xianshou* states, "Mantras are the secret doctrine of all buddhas, which cannot be comprehended by practicing Buddhists. One needs only to recite them - not understand them."

The *Surangama Sutra* states, "The secret doctrine of the mantras of all buddhas is only known and understood between buddhas, for their meanings cannot be readily penetrated by other sages. However, by reciting these mantras, karmic transgressions are eradicated and buddhahood is swiftly attained."

I shall quote a simple example:

When we are sick, we consult a doctor. The doctor prescribes us an effective medication, but he would not reveal the chemical compound of the medication, like how much protein, zinc, iron, amino acids there are, and so on. The doctor only prescribes us the medicine. And when we take the medicine, we are healed.

Today, the mantras of Vajrayana may not be understood by all sentient beings and all bodhisattvas in the causal stage of bodhisattvahood. But as long as you keep to the recitation, you shall board the Dharma ship, and find your body and mind being transformed into the Dharmakaya of Vairocana. You shall travel across the Ocean of Samantabhadra, liberated from life and death naturally and attain the omnipresent fruition of buddhahood.

Let me say this. Mantra itself is neither arising nor ceasing, has no form nor is formless, neither taken nor abandoned. It attaches the highest and most supreme meaning to all Dharma, and displays the truth of the tranquility of non-causation, non-abiding nirvana, and the truth of non-verbal and non-written doctrine. Thus mantras are not to be translated. The *Prajnaparamita Sutra* states, "Dharani is like a wonderful medicine, much like the celestial nectar. It can heal all illnesses, and all who consume this medicine constantly shall receive peace of mind."

67. OM BU LIN

Someone asked me, "What mantra is OM BU LIN?"

I replied, "This mantra is the one syllable heart mantra mentioned in the *Manjushri Sadhana Sutra*. It is also known as the Great Wheel One Syllable Mantra, whose pronunciation is BU LIN [Sanskrit syllable: BHRUM]." The person asked again, "Why do we need to recite this mantra after completing cultivation of the True Buddha Tantra?"

I replied, "According to Buddhist scriptures, when an individual worries that he may not have much success with his recitation of mantras and his cultivation of Vajrayana practices, he may complete his practice by ending with this mantra, and he shall be assured of accomplishment. If no results are seen, the guardian of this mantra shall experience a major crack on his head. Therefore, this mantra indeed can help all other mantras achieve their intended results swiftly."

Question: "What is the merit of this OM BU LIN mantra?"

My reply: "Besides facilitating the swift ripening of all mantra accomplishments, if a person recites this mantra, all evil spirits within a square area, with each side as long as five hundred ancient Chinese horse relay stations, would flee instantly. Even the deities of evil stars and all celestial maras would not dare come near. This mantra acts like a wish-fulfilling pearl which can fulfill all wishes. It can subjugate ferocious demons and destroy all evil mantras in the world. It offers the comfort of fearlessness to all sentient beings and gives them joy and happiness."

Question: "How is it that OM BU LIN can attract such great merits?"

My reply: "This OM BU LIN mantra is the heart of Manjushri Bodhisattva, and is the supreme crown of all buddhas."

The Great Wheel One Syllable Mantra is actually BU LIN. OM means homage. BU LIN is the main mantra itself. I received the transmission of this mantra from Vajra Master Pufang. The reason for placing this mantra at the end of the True Buddha Tantra practice was mainly to help speed up the ripening of all results and accomplishments of all mantras. Therefore, we should give our thanks to Vajra Master Pufang for his transmission.

I was also asked why there is a need to recite OM MANI PADME HUM after reciting OM BU LIN three times. Let me explain that the Six-Syllable Mantra is well known to many, and to understand this mantra, you may read up on it in the *Karandavyuha Sutra*. Reciting this mantra at the end is simply to swiftly ripen the fruition of the bodhisattva, as the mantra holds the key to infinite states of samadhi.

I can say that the whole of Tibet is chanting OM MANI PADME HUM.

68. The Authenticity of the Personal Deity

Those who follow Zen Buddhism often have the notion that during meditation, if you see the Buddha or any patriarch approaching, you should regard it as the presence of an evil being or simply an illusion, which must be dismissed as falsehood. Thus, there is the saying "When you meet the Buddha, kill him. When you meet the mara, kill him."

Zen Buddhism regards the Vajrayana approach to establishing mandalas, forming mudras and chanting mantras as attachment to form. Zen Buddhism views itself as the formless Dharma gate, and upon seeing a cultivator of mantra, the Zen practitioner often slanders the Vajrayana cultivator as Zen does not see mantra recitation as proper cultivation.

Yet, this is what I have to say. In the endless Dharma Realms, there already exist infinite Dharma gates, and the formless gate is but one of the countless gates. The Dharma gate of Amitabha Buddha's Western Pure Land of Ultimate Bliss is one, and Maitreya Bodhisattva's tower shall be the Dharma gate of the future. In the view of Vajrayana Buddhism, every Buddha who attains buddhahood and delivers sentient beings accomplishes this through the practice of mantra. This is the gate of "revealing truth through respective manifestations of activities" as described in the "Ten Mysterious Gates" [of the Huayan School of Buddhism].

Therefore, in the view of Vajrayana Buddhism, if you see the personal deity appearing in your meditation, dream, or in the waking hours, and the personal deity radiates light towards you, touches your head, gives precious objects, or offers medicinal pills, these are signs of enhancement of your blessings and wisdom. Thus, you should not have doubts, for these are auspicious signs. We are here to teach you not to be attached to what you see, and to refrain from developing thoughts of taking and rejecting, as we need to view these spiritual occurrences as means of encouragement. In this way, the practitioner avoids being drawn into the mara realms due to attachment.

If the Vajrayana practitioner sees the personal deity and suspects that it is an illusory manifestation of the maras, what should the practitioner do? Let me teach you how to resolve this. When the personal deity appears, and the practitioner is unsure of its authenticity, he or she may recite the Root Guru's Mantra three times: OM GURU LIAN SHENG SIDDHI HUM and validate its identity.

If it is a manifestation of the mara, it will immediately vanish. If it is an authentic personal deity, it shall appear even clearer than before. Another way is to empty yourself of the attachment to the self, and at this point, the mara's manifested deity should vanish as well.

149

69. Mudra as Transmitted from Space

A mudra is a seal formed with your fingers. It symbolizes the equanimity and non-difference that exist between the mind of a Buddha and the true nature of all sentient beings. The secret mudras that are being transmitted in Vajrayana Buddhism are embedded with hidden meanings. The ten fingers represent the ten Dharma Realms, and they also symbolize the five elements of earth, water, fire, wind and space.

Another interpretation suggests:

The thumb - the Wisdom of Ultimate Reality.

The index finger - the Great Mirror-like Wisdom.

The middle finger - the Wisdom of Equanimity.

The ring finger - the Wisdom of Discriminatory Awareness.

The little finger - the All-accomplishing Wisdom.

The right hand's formation of a mudra represents blessings, whereas the left hand's formation of a mudra represents wisdom. When I first learned to form mudras, they were transmitted to me by my spiritual teacher, the Eminent Sanshan-Jiuhou, who resided in space. I was seated in meditation with my palms placed together. Gradually, my fingers began to bend, straighten and turn automatically, and in so doing, formed different kinds of mudras.

Thus, many of the mudras found in True Buddha School were first transmitted from space. This is true. I, Living Buddha Lian-sheng, Sheng-yen Lu am not making this up. My mudras were indeed transmitted directly to me from space. When I was studying these mudras, I found them amazing and incredible, as they could transform freely in many unexpected variations. It was simply magical and extraordinary.

Back then, the Eminent Sanshan-Jiuhou told me, "A mudra connects the mind to the body. In this way, the body reflects the mind. As the body and mind become one, its transformations are endless."

When the mudra is connected with the heart, nothing shall stand in the way. When I later learned of the "heart of heart mudra," I instantly realized that when I formed this mudra, and made contact, I would directly touch the heart of the personal deity. At this moment, the heart of the practitioner and the heart of the personal deity are interconnected.

Let me say this. When your hands form the mudra, it creates a matrix of adamantine adornment that emits infinite streams of light, illuminating all of creation!

70. Essentials of Vajrayana Cultivation

Vajrayana practice involves the preparatory procedures, the main procedures, and the concluding procedures. Here are the essentials of the main procedures of Vajrayana practice. The practitioner sits before the personal deity at the mandala shrine, forms the deity's mudra and visualizes the deity appearing clearly in front of the practitioner in an elevated position. The personal deity radiates brilliant light that illuminates all sentient beings of the ten Dharma Realms. Once illuminated by the radiance of the deity's bodhicitta, countless eons of transgressions, karma, mara hindrances, illnesses and calamities weighing on these sentient beings are removed and eliminated. All sentient beings of the ten Dharma Realms shall generate bodhicitta and practice the path of bodhisattvahood and buddhahood.

Next, visualize all sentient beings of the ten Dharma Realms, each transforming into the personal deity, each radiating lights, then combine to form a single personal deity before the practitioner. The personal deity radiates light towards the practitioner, empowering him so that all his past eons of transgressions, karma and mara hindrances, illnesses and calamities are transformed into streams of dark energy which are released through the pores of the skin. The practitioner shall generate bodhicitta, and practice the path of bodhisattvahood and buddhahood.

Next, visualize the personal deity entering into the central channel through the top of the crown of the practitioner, and sits on the lotus located at the heart chakra of the practitioner. The deity radiates light, and enlarges to the exact size of the practitioner. In an instant, the practitioner is the deity, and the deity is the practitioner, with the two of them being one and the same.

Release the mudra by touching the head. Recite the deity's mantra one hundred and eight times or more, or one thousand and eighty times. The more recitations chanted, the better.

When you complete your recitation, form the Samaya Meditation Mudra, and imagine yourself entering into the seed syllable OM. The syllable OM then enters into a moon disc. The moon disc shrinks into a drop of light which shoots straight into space and merges with space. Beyond space there is no existence of body and mind. I am space, and space is me. The Tathagata, the Thus Come One, remains in constant stillness and non-abiding.

I teach my True Buddha disciples how to visualize and cultivate in this way, practicing once a day or three times a day. It is the most supreme form of the main procedures in Vajrayana practice. The main procedures include visualization, mantra recitation, and entering into samadhi.

71. The Padmakumara Mudra and the Method of Using the Bell and Vajra

The origin of the mudra of Padmakumara, one of the personal deities of True Buddha School, stems from an occasion when Living Buddha Lian-sheng entered into the deity samadhi and automatically formed the mudra. The right hand gesture signifies the expounding of Dharma while the left hand indicates the holding of a lotus.

The Dharma Expounding Mudra symbolizes the fluent elucidation of all dharma while the Lotus Holding Mudra represents the purity of the six senses, with the purity of body, speech and mind as uncontaminated as the lotus.

Someone asked, "Since Padmakumara is Padmakumara, why is he also the transformation of Amitabha Buddha?"

Let me clarify this. Take Avalokitesvara Bodhisattva (Guanyin) as an example. This bodhisattva has many emanation bodies. The Six Guanyin Bodhisattvas are: the Thousand-armed Guanyin, the Sacred Guanyin, the Horse Headed Guanyin [or Hayagriva], the Eleven-headed Kannon [or Ekadasamukha], Cundi Guanyin, and Nyoirin-kannon [or Cintamani-cakra]. Avalokitesvara Bodhisattva is known

to have thirty-two manifested bodies, and is capable of infinite transformations. It is indeed inconceivable.

As for Padmakumara, he is born out of Vairocana Tathagata, abides
in Buddha Locana, and is manifested through Amitabha Buddha. You
can say that he is the combined manifestation of Vairocana Tathagata,
Buddha Locana and Amitabha Buddha, and thus the lineage is even
more extraordinary.

Another person asked, "The method of using the bell and vajra in
True Buddha School is different from that of Tibetan Buddhism and
Shingon Buddhism. Why?"

My reply was that when I entered into the samadhi of my personal
deity, I entered the heart of Vajrasattva, and as I was holding the bell
and vajra in my hands, I was transformed into Vajrapani Bodhisattva.
When Vajrapani Bodhisattva moved the bell and vajra, the method
was transmitted.

The reason it differs from others is that the method of using the bell
and vajra is transmitted through a spiritual lineage, but not from a human lineage. Included in the True Buddha Tantra and the teachings of
other Vajrayana schools are the common and uncommon practices.
Since the Padmakumara Siddhi (Pure Land), the Padmakumara deity, its mudra, mantra, and the method of using the bell and vajra are
available only in True Buddha School, it can be said that they form an
uncommon practice.

Since the practice of the Padmakumara personal deity is an uncommon practice, it is a rare practice indeed.

72. Mantras are the Infinite Dharma Treasury of All Buddhas

When the Buddha expounded the Dharma, he taught both the Sutrayana and Vajrayana teachings. The Sutrayana teachings touch widely on the principles of Buddhism and the nature of phenomena. It enlightens one on the subjects of emptiness and existence, through which one cultivates and attains the Truth Body [or Dharmakaya], and arrives at the other shore. The Vajrayana teachings emphasize the recitation of secret mantras with little explanation, yet they lead one to attain buddhahood at once.

When I first started studied mantras, my teacher Reverend Liaoming related to me two incredible and incomprehensible examples.

The first example: When cultivating the rice offering practice, the Vajrayana practitioner holds the rice in his hand, and upon completion of the mandala offering mantra, he casts the rice as a spiritual offering. If a bird consumes the rice, which has been blessed by the power of mantra, the bird shall attain buddhahood in a future life.

The second example: If a person walks under a temple's wooden sign inscribed with the Six-Syllable Mantra, and it happens that the wind blows the dust off the wooden board and the dust falls onto the person, the person's karma shall be removed completely. The seed of bodhi shall be planted into his heart and in a future life this individual shall definitely attain buddhahood.

When these two examples were related to me, they really made a strong impression in my mind. Mantras are the very essence and body of the secret Dharma Realm. It has inconceivable effects when applied through the actions of the Three Secrets. It is the most supreme vehicle of all Dharma. Mantra belongs in the Dharma Realm of the formless, through which all buddhas are born. It houses immeasurable Dharma treasures.

When I read the *Dharani Pitaka* [the Buddhist Canon of Mantras], I discovered this:

The Buddha, in his compassion for future sentient beings, spoke of the mantras. If Buddhist practitioners accept and recite these mantras, their karma of ten thousand, a million, or infinite kalpas, including karma of the Five Unpardonable Transgressions [Five Avici Sins], will be completely eliminated.

Should anyone recite mantras, all bodhisattvas shall become his or her good companions. The practitioner shall have the opportunity to meet all buddhas wherever he or she is born, and the individual's cultivation shall be accelerated towards attaining Supreme Perfect Enlightenment.

If sentient beings whose merits and blessings are few, and whose natural capacity to cultivate the Dharma and their Bodhyanga [factors of enlightenment] are literally non-existent, decide to recite a Buddha's mantra just once, these sentient beings shall be instantly blessed with the growth of their capacity for enlightenment. Therefore, by reciting mantras diligently, they would definitely attain buddhahood based on the merits of their effort.

It is said in the *Dharani Pitaka* that by reciting mantras, the thousands of actions from the Six Perfections shall be naturally complete.

73. Mantras are a Treasury of Meditation

In this short article, I shall reveal "The Practice of Casting Light with Mantra and Entering into Samadhi." This practice is rarely transmitted in public, and that makes it extremely precious. The practitioner forms the mudra of his personal deity and visualizes his personal deity entering into himself. In an instant, he is transformed into the deity with all the thirty-two major marks and eighty minor marks of a buddha, displaying a perfect aura of light. He then visualizes himself touching his crown chakra with the deity's mudra and plants the syllable OM. Then he touches his throat chakra to plant the syllable AH, touches his heart chakra to plant the syllable HUM, touches his navel chakra to plant the syllable SO and finally touches his root chakra to plant the syllable HA [all syllables in Sanskrit letters for this particular visualization].

The syllable OM is planted at the crown chakra; its color is white, radiating infinite light to remove all karmic hindrances.

The syllable AH is planted at the throat chakra; its color is red, illuminating all dense darkness to generate the wisdom of the Tathagata.

The syllable HUM is planted at the heart chakra; its color is blue, like pure lapis lazuli, speeding the cultivator towards the other shore.

The syllable SO is planted at the navel chakra; its color is yellow, seated on the vajra throne, it swiftly turns the Dharma wheel.

The syllable HA is planted at the root chakra; it color is green. All is auspicious and complete, swiftly bringing the cultivator to the state of Nirvana.

By planting the seed syllables and visualizing the respective color of light, the cultivator forms the truth body of the personal deity. In doing so, all past karmic transgression are removed and one receives blessings, great wisdom and purity. Visualizing the seed syllables and colors in this way helps one enter samadhi quickly and arrive at the siddhi of the personal deity. This is due to the incredible inherent nature of each mantra syllable.

Mantra in its true origin is "unborn," and thus has neither a beginning nor an end; and as such, nothing is attained. Therefore, it is not subject to creation and destruction, and so is not subject to defilement. As it is not defiled, supreme awareness is gained. Furthermore, there is nothing to differentiate, so one is left in a state of equanimity. In this state, one rises beyond cause and effect and enters into absolute truth, thereby validating the True Suchness of the Dharma Realm. This is entering into samadhi. Let me draw your attention to the above paragraph, as it illustrates the stages of entering into samadhi, beginning with "the origin is unborn" and progressing to validating the True Suchness of the Dharma Realm. The *Great Compassion Dharani Sutra* states, "Dharani is the treasury of meditation, as hundreds and thousands of samadhi states often manifest through it."

74. Aspiring the Greatest Bodhicitta

When I first attained Enlightenment, I made the following vow: "Never shall I abandon a single sentient being." And with this vow came the vow "May I deliver all sentient beings even if I have to shatter into a thousand pieces." When this bodhicitta was first generated, heaven and earth trembled and shook violently.

I am aware that when the Buddha first started to deliver sentient beings, he avoided ordaining women as nuns and forbade his disciples from bringing their wives and children along to hear his discourses. The Buddha set down various precepts such as refraining from killing, committing lascivious acts, and consuming alcohol. The Buddha warned his disciples, "A person who indulges in sexual lust will never attain buddhahood, for there is no need to have a wife. A person who indulges in killing will never attain buddhahood, for there is no need to consume the flesh of sentient beings. A person who is in a disoriented state will never attain buddhahood, for there is no need to consume fine alcoholic drinks."

From this, we know that the Buddhist precepts and codes are extremely strict. Hence, when faced with the massive numbers of sentient beings, you can only deliver those who are willing and able.

Those who are not willing and able you would have to leave alone.

Nonetheless, I made the vow: "Never shall I abandon a single sentient being." With this vow, there is no discrimination between the defiled and the pure, and no questioning of whether one is a lay Buddhist or an ordained monk, married or single, male or female, involved with killing or not, vegetarian or non-vegetarian, and so on. This is because it is all too common to find mundane men of this age attached to their wives and children, indulging in wining and dining. Such habits are difficult to correct. If someone does not reach out to deliver them, when would they ever find the opportunity to cultivate the Buddhadharma? When would they ever find liberation from samsara? In fact, people like this comprise the vast majority of the people in this mundane world.

Therefore, I say to you:

You are permitted to have a wife, but you must refrain from sexual misconduct.

You are permitted to consume meat, but you must recite the deliverance mantra, and cultivate the deliverance practice.

You are permitted to consume wine, but you must drink in moderation, without getting drunk and losing control of yourself.

Therefore, I say that I can allow my disciples to pursue political positions and social status, to seek wealth and honor, to fulfill the wish of having a family, to seek riches of gold and jewels, cars and houses, to seek good health and longevity, and seek all that constitute the happiness of life.

This is done in the name of "Never shall I abandon a single sentient being." I made these allowances to fulfill the wishes of sentient beings, as I want to make things as easy as possible for the deliverance of sentient beings, never wanting to turn any away.

I wish that you can understand this and make spiritual progress in your cultivation and mantra recitation.

75. The Protection Method and the Boundary Method

When Vajrayana practitioner engages in the cultivation of any Vajrayana practices, the protection practice and boundary practice are very important. If you do not set a boundary around your mandala shrine and engage in a protection practice, the maras will eat you for breakfast.

In True Buddha School, we teach the practice of Armor Protection. During every practice session, the practitioner forms the Vajra Mudra, chants the heart mantra of Vajrapani Bodhisattva, and then touches the forehead with the mudra, followed by the throat, the heart, the left shoulder, and the right shoulder. This creates the Armor Protection.

The practitioner may also take threads of string weaved together by young children (or strings purified over fire). Recite the Vajra Mantra once and tie a knot. Complete twenty-one knots, and hang the string of knots around your neck or tie it around your arm. This can protect you from all evil spirits and demons. Thus, this is also a method of protection.

All protective strings and protective amulets have protection power. It is best to recite the mantra twenty-one times every two weeks and pray to the dharma protectors to once again empower the strings and amulets. If you do this, they shall be effective.

When the practitioner sets a boundary in the mandala shrine, he may use a bottle of pure water or perfume, and offer it at the mandala shrine. He should recite the dharma protector's mantra one hundred and eight times or one thousand and eighty times. He should visualize the protector radiating light to bless the pure water or perfume. He should take the perfume and sprinkle it in all ten directions around the shrine to set the boundary. Within the confines of the sprinkled region, no evil spirits and demons would dare enter.

This boundary method is suitable for the mandala shrine, or for the house. You can even set a boundary around larger land areas with this method. But to achieve results you need to strengthen this boundary by doing the practice once every two weeks.

Some have used this protection method on the body of a patient, spraying the perfume onto the body and reciting the vajra protector's mantra. The patient may react with a loud cry and any illness due to the possession of evil spirits and demons shall be healed immediately. If one should choose the Day of Removal ["chu ri"] as designated on the Chinese lunar calendar, it would yield even better results.

76. The Method of Seeing All Spiritual Beings

Someone asked me, "You, Living Buddha Lian-sheng, can see all spirits. Why is it that you can see them, and we can't?"

I smiled and said, "The reason I can see them is because when I was twenty-six years old, the Golden Mother of the Jade Pond opened my divine eye. You must be built with a certain inborn quality before you can see all spirits. Otherwise, you need to cultivate diligently, so that when the time comes, you will see them."

"How do you cultivate the divine eye?"

I replied, "When you open your heart chakra, radiating soft white light, your divine eye shall open. You shall see infinite buddhas and bodhisattvas who are your close companions. You can travel to all the pure lands of the buddhas and listen to their teachings in person."

I added, "In the Vajrayana practice of cultivating vital winds, channels and drops, opening the central channel is followed by the opening of the five chakras. This is the standard way of cultivating the opening of the divine eye."

"Are there other Vajrayana practices that enable you to see all spirits?"

"Indeed there are other Vajrayana practices for seeing all spirits.

You need to use Niuhuang [ox gallstone, dried and made into powder or pills]. Recite the mantra of Cundi Bodhisattva. You need to recite until you see the Niuhuang turning into 'smoke' or 'fire.' Then rub the Niuhuang over your eyes and consume it, and you shall immediately see all spirits."

I added, "To my knowledge, if a practitioner circumambulates the bodhi tree clockwise, recites the heart mantra of Shakyamuni Buddha a million times, and prays to the Buddha to empower his divine eye, he shall immediately see buddhas, bodhisattvas and arhats appearing before him where they shall expound the Dharma to him."

In the past, I taught the method of seeing your deceased ancestors. The method goes like this: Obtain a few drops of tears from any deceased person and mix the tears with perfume. Offer this mixture in the mandala shrine, and begin reciting mantra until you see a glow over the perfume. Take the perfume and rub it on your eyelids and you shall immediately see your ancestors and all other spirits.

Do not be alarmed or frightened when you start seeing spirits. Consider it a natural occurrence, and maintain an attitude of non-attachment and non-delusion. From the experiences of seeing the spirit world, the practitioner will be able to understand how things really work; how every fortune and misfortune is based on good and bad deeds committed. He shall be forewarned of any trouble or problem that comes his way.

If you persevere in your cultivation to see all spirits, it is not a difficult thing to achieve!

77. Signs of Purification as Arisen from the Repentance Practice

Many people have asked me, "When cultivating the repentance practice, how do you know if your bad karma has been removed?"

I replied, "Watch for the signs of repentance."

I once told my disciples that if they see their personal deity appearing to touch their heads while they are cultivating the repentance practice, it means that the buddhas and bodhisattvas have forgiven their misdeeds. It means that they have received a sign of repentance.

Many disciples, upon the completion of their repentance practice, dreamed of many tiny worms falling off when they combed their hair. This is another validation of receiving a sign of repentance.

One disciple had a dream of flying towards space, bathing himself in the purity of the universe, cleansing himself of all dirt and impurities. This is also a sign of repentance.

Other signs of repentance include dreams and visions of consuming white objects and vomiting dark objects; black worms crawling out of your pores; the personal deity giving you a discourse; swallowing the sun or moon; chasing away a black ox or a bad tempered horse; ascending to the lion's throne; entering into the palaces of bud-dhas and bodhisattvas; seeing your body emit white light; your body having a fragrant scent; ascending a white mountain and riding on a dharma ship across the great ocean, and so on.

When a person recites the Vajrasattva Hundred Syllable Mantra ten thousand times and still does not see any sign of repentance, he may want to recite up to twenty thousand times. If he still does not see any sign of repentance, he must then recite up to seven hundred thousand times. This is an indication that the individual has commit-ted the Five Unpardonable Transgressions [Five Avici Sins] in his past lives. However, if he completes seven hundred thousand recitations, he shall see the signs of repentance.

There are many repentance practices in Buddhism, in both the Sutrayana and Vajrayana teachings. In the Sutrayana system, repen-tance practices include the Liang Emperor Repentance, the Water Re-pentance, the Great Compassion Repentance, the Lotus Repentance [from the *Lotus Sutra*], and so on. The main repentance practice found in Vajrayana Buddhism is the Vajrasattva Hundred Syllable Mantra Practice. When a person recites this mantra, he transforms all nega-tive karma into emptiness, and dissolves all transgression into space.

There was this one individual who used to slander Living Buddha Lian-sheng, Sheng-yen Lu, and later realized his mistakes and took refuge in True Buddha School. As he was cultivating the Vajrasattva Practice, he saw a black snake being vomited from his mouth. Af-ter this experience, he saw great improvement in his cultivation, and presently his spiritual conviction is firm and his attainment is excel-lent.

When we sincerely repent, the buddhas and bodhisattvas, out of their compassion for us, will reveal to us the signs of repentance.

78. The Art of Knowing the Future

Someone asked me, "Can you see into the future?"
I replied, "Sure."
"If you know a disaster awaits you, can you avert it?"
I replied, "You can do your best to avert it, but your chances of success still hinge on your destiny."
"Are there methods in the teachings of Vajrayana where we can see into the future?"
I replied, "There are many ways!"
I shall share one practice with you. Take a mirror; purify it over fire before hanging it in your mandala shrine. Then obtain some fragrant flowers and recite your personal deity's mantra one hundred and eight times to bless and empower the flowers. Then take each flower and again recite the deity mantra once and cast the flower towards the mirror. Do this twenty-one or forty-nine times. Sit up straight and look into the mirror. The mirror shall reveal writings to inform you about your future.
Based on the above principle, you may choose a clean bowl instead of a mirror. Fill the bowl with clean water. First recite your personal deity's mantra one hundred and eight times to bless and empower the

flowers, then with each additional recitation of mantra, take a flower petal and cast it into the bowl of water. Repeat this twenty-one or forty-nine times. Look into the bowl of water and pay attention to the writings that appear. You will be told what you wish to know about your future.

Acting on the same principle, you can choose a pure crystal ball and purify it over the fire at the mandala shrine. The practitioner should recite the personal deity's mantra one hundred and eight times to bless and empower the flowers. Then, with each additional recitation of the mantra, take a petal and cast it at the crystal ball. Do this twenty-one times or forty-nine times. Look into the crystal ball and it shall reveal words or images which will tell you what you wish to know about your future.

However, I do not need to resort to these practices. When I go to bed, I just pray to my personal deity. Once I shut my eyes, a white spot shall appear, eventually forming a white screen. Events in the future will be projected onto this screen, just like watching a movie. Today I see no meaning in knowing the future. It is better not to know anything, for any foreknowledge of things brings early fear.

Do your Vajrayana cultivation sincerely, and rise above all afflictions. Go with the flow and know that self-liberation from life and death must always come first!

79. Healing with Vajrayana Techniques

I was twenty-six years old when I was blessed with the fortune of having my divine eye opened by the Golden Mother of the Jade Pond and subsequently received the transmission of the "Shang Letter Talisman" and the "Ghost Letter Talisman" from Taoist Master Qing-zhen. I also received Vajrayana transmission from other masters, and I became well known.

During my stay in Taiwan, I changed residences several times to avoid drawing too much attention. As I had attained spiritual resonance with my Vajrayana practice, I was able to see into the future and heal all kinds of illnesses with great success. As my reputation spread by word of mouth, people by the hundreds flocked to me for consultation everyday, leaving me no choice but to keep moving house. I once professed that the mental patients who were healed by my use of Vajrayana mantras and Taoist talismans could fill a whole train. Some psychiatrists even told the patients' family members to consult Grand Master Sheng-yen Lu.

At that time, a long line of parked cars was always present outside my house, often as long as a kilometer. Not only was I no longer able to handle the crowds, but my neighbors couldn't stand it anymore either. The situation only improved after I moved to America.

If a mental patient is suffering from the disturbance of spiritual entities, a practitioner may obtain a willow stick or kusha grass, empower it by reciting a mantra one hundred and eight times or one thousand and eighty times, and use the stick or grass to brush the mental patient with it. The spiritual entities shall immediately leave the patient. If the patient lives far away or for some reason is unable to personally come for a healing, the practitioner can use a piece of paper placed in front of the shrine, and draw the outline of a human form representing the patient. Write down the patient's name and his or her date of birth. Recite the mantra, and use a pomegranate stick to hit the patient's figure on the paper. The spiritual entity that has possessed the patient will no longer be able to cling onto the patient and the patient shall recover after the spirit exits his or her body.

The Shang Letter Talismans as transmitted by the Taoist Master Qingzhen are used with great success and can heal a thousand illnesses. Once a talisman is used, the illness is removed. If there is a very grave illness, it is best to conduct a homa (fire offering) practice, during which "white offerings" or milk can be cast into the flame. When chanting the mantra, do include the patient's name. Once spiritual resonance occurs, even a grave illness can be reversed.

I once had an illness which no doctors could diagnose and no medication could cure. As a last resort, I drew three Ghost Letter Talismans, recited the appropriate mantra, and prayed to the Golden Mother of the Jade Pond. I burned the talismans and consumed the ashes with water. A miracle happened and I was completely healed. I am telling the truth. Talismans and mantras can heal illnesses. It is simply incredible!

80. The Secret of Entering Celestial Palaces

Any Vajrayana practitioner who has been practicing for some time may long for a glimpse of celestial palaces, or wish to enter dragon palaces, asura palaces, or the adobe of the great mountain gods, but denied the experience.

In the early days of my training, Vajra Master Sakya Zhengkong secretly imparted such a method to me which is detailed as follows:

The practitioner should obtain a five or seven story stupa (or pagoda) of any size and then build a mandala around the stupa. Make an offering of flowers to the stupa, as you can afford, and recite a certain mantra with the hands forming the root mudra. Circumambulate the stupa in a clockwise manner and recite the mantra up to six hundred thousand times. Use the root mudra to touch the stupa. Touch the stupa seven times with the root mudra, and recite the mantra seven times. Then recite these words:

> With these seven root mudras
> Release the seal to the sixteen senior beings
> As the Iron Gate of Southern India opens
> The practitioner shall find his way in.

("The sixteen senior beings" refer to the sixteen bodhisattvas in the

Vajradhatu Mandala.)

On that very night, the personal deity shall appear and lead the practitioner into the celestial palaces or dragon palaces, or asura palaces, or the abodes of the great mountain gods, and upon entering the palaces, the practitioner shall be rewarded with wonderful nectar or dharma medicinal pills, perhaps receive a precious Vajrayana practice, or a personal discourse given by a bodhisattva. It would be most extraordinary.

I remember I once traveled alone to Japan, and upon arriving at Lake Kawaguchi, the place was raining non-stop that evening, and the inn was filled to capacity. I felt lost at this inn which was situated at Lake Kawaguchi beneath Mount Fuji. Fortunately, the inn's receptionist found me a temporary room reserved for the caretakers. That night, I entered into the abode of the God of Mount Fuji and received a grand reception from the mountain god himself. I had in fact stayed in the grand palace of the God of Mount Fuji. This was a result of having practiced the method of entering celestial palaces. When you gain entrance into the celestial palaces, if you wish for purification, enhancement, harmonization, or subjugation, your wish shall be fulfilled. Everything shall be auspicious.

81. The Method of Touching the Head and Slapping the Back

Someone observed the way I performed healings, such as how I would place my hand on the patient's head or instruct the patient to turn around so that I could slap his back with my hand. Upon completion, I would say that the illness was healed.

The curious observer asked, "How is it that, by touching the head and patting the back, an illness can be healed?" I replied, "Well, Vajrayana is like that."

Some of these patients were healed on the spot while others needed another day before they recovered. This touching of the head and slapping of the back is simply marvelous! Actually, to arrive at this level of achievement requires a long period of training, and it cannot be attained overnight. Think about this: I, Living Buddha Lian-sheng, Sheng-yen Lu have been consistently and diligently reciting the mantras, and the Buddha's name, cultivating, performing homa, purifying myself, giving mandala offerings, and practicing generosity for the past thirty years without fail. I am always with my personal deity, and my guru always resides above my crown. The dharma protectors guard and surround me in circles, and all buddhas, bodhisattvas and the eight divisions of spiritual beings often descend wherever I go.

When I place my hand on a patient's head, or slap a patient's back, I would have already quietly recited the mantra OM AH HUM, which empowers my hand, and in turn blesses the patient. Therefore, when I touch the patient, his or her illness is relieved. And when I slap the patient's back, all spiritual entities will detach themselves from the patient immediately, and the patient is cured of his or her illness.

I have the strongest spiritual conviction, always doing my cultivation and following the precepts without fail. The celestial maras may use all means to dissuade me from my path, but I always keep going. Thus, I always have the respect, support, and blessings of the devas.

I want to offer again this advice to all my disciples:

Follow the precepts, keep up with your recitations, and act according to the teachings. Never lose your spiritual conviction; be determined to reach fruition, swiftly attaining Supreme Perfect Enlightenment.

82. The Practice of Harmonization

The karma yogas of purification, enhancement, harmonization and subjugation are generally categorized as worldly activities. I have written in great length about these four yogas in my books, so I will not repeat that here.

When I provide help to sentient beings, I observe that the pain felt when the family is in disharmony is no less than the pain felt when a person is sick. This is when the husband and wife are not happy with each other, cannot get along and desert each other. The afflictions caused by such disharmony are painful beyond words.

In the past, when I helped others cultivate the practice of harmonization, I employed these two approaches:

Obtain a red string and offer it at the mandala shrine. Recite a mantra and cultivate the Vajrayana practice. During the recitation of mantra, include the names of the married couple. If for example one is cultivating the Kurukulle Practice, one would need to recite it this way: "OM KURUKULLE HRIH. I decree XX and XX to have fulfillment of harmonization, SOHA."

The Vajrayana cultivation must be done in accordance to the sadhana of the practice of harmonization, and the red strings must be empowered. Practice it for seven sessions, twenty-one sessions or forty-nine sessions. Then obtain one shoe each from the married couple, the left shoe from the husband and the right shoe from the wife, tie them together with the red string and place the shoes under the couple's bed. In this way, the couple shall gain mutual respect and love for each other.

The second approach will remarkably reverse a marriage crisis. If the marriage has deteriorated seriously, it will require the use of a harmonization homa. The harmonization practice can renew a marital relationship, and help the couple conceive a baby.

The wish for a son or daughter and a good affectionate marriage can be fulfilled through Vajrayana practices. They can bring great fulfillment to the activities of this world and those beyond.

83. The Practice of Subjugation

Someone said, "The subjugation practice of Vajrayana Buddhism is no different from the spell casting practice of Voodoo!"

Then the person added, "The subjugation practice brings only harm to people, causing them to contract cancer and tumors, encounter accidents, die in a car crash, and so on."

Such opinions may seem terrifying, but in reality it is far from the truth. The subjugation practice of Vajrayana is performed to subjugate all evil spiritual entities, ferocious dragons and beasts that harm all living beings. It is also used to subjugate all evil men who cause harm to countries and their people, including those who have betrayed the truth, have caused destruction to the Three Jewels and mantras, or have created hindrances to those who recite mantras. Such evil men shall be dealt with by the mantra practitioner whose great compassion is exercised through cultivating the subjugation practice.

In the tantras it is said, "If you cultivate the subjugation practice to settle a personal score or do so out of selfish desires, you shall meet with misfortune." This explains that the subjugation practice has to be cultivated for the good of all and not for settling personal scores and dealing with enemies. It adds, "If an evil man is feeling unsettled in his body and mind, is down with a grave illness, or near the brink of death, we must advise him to mend his ways and repent. If repentance is genuine, we should chant for him to bring about purification so that he avoids any calamity."

Let me say that the cultivation of subjugation practice must be accompanied by great compassion.

1. Cultivate it for the good of all.
2. Cultivate it to deliver evil men.

The subjugation practice of Vajrayana is definitely far from what is being circulated by the uninitiated, which is that it is the same as the spell casting magic of Voodoo. The subjugation practice of Vajrayana is not meant to harm others, but intended to save them from further transgressions.

When cultivating the subjugation practice, you must include these syllables in the mantra:

[transliteration] hum hum hum fazha

[Sanskrit] HUM HUM HUM PHAT.

The body mudra of the subjugation practice is rather unique in that it requires you to crouch, with the left foot pressed against the right foot.

I, Living Buddha Lian-sheng, Sheng-yen Lu have never used the subjugation practice for the sole reason that I like to let things take their natural course. The Law of Cause and Effect is always at work, and whatever that comes shall come, and whatever that leaves shall leave. I simply let things be.

84. The Way of Receiving Great Wisdom

Once at Sarnath in India, my disciples and I paid homage and prostrated at the foot of the Relics Stupa where Shakyamu-ni Buddha first turned the Dharma wheel. Before the stupa, Geshe Lobsang Tenzin and other lamas prepared the offerings of one hundred and eight candle sticks, as well as flowers, incense, lights, tea and fruits. My disciples and I cultivated a session of Vajrayana practice in front of the Relics Stupa. This place was where the Buddha first de-livered and expounded on the Four Noble Truths to the five ascetics.

Before cultivation, we circumambulated the stupa in a clockwise manner, reciting mantras as we walked. I chanted the Guru's Heart Mantra. After completing the session of cultivation, we entered into meditation while forming mudras and reciting mantras. We visual-ized the respective Sanskrit syllable and aligned our body, speech and mind as one.

With my mind cleared, I visualized a Sanskrit syllable RAM appear-ing at the top of my crown, which radiated light like the full moon. I recited the syllable OM twenty-one times. This is a mantra to purify the Dharma Realms, and purify all three karmas of body, speech and mind. It eliminates all karmic hindrances. It can accomplish all virtuous deeds, for when one is purified, so are the Dharma Realms of the ten directions.

At that time, I saw the Buddha Eye, which is the eye of Shakyamuni Buddha. It appeared flawless and brilliant, its wonderful features beyond any verbal or written description. It was truly extraordinary.

The eye of the Tathagata is luminous, pure and spotless. Like a mani pearl, its light is perfect and filled with awareness. The Buddha Eye shined the light of the wonderful lotus [symbolizing the Buddha's wisdom] upon me as I sat upright in my meditation. In an instant, its wisdom cut away all hindrances, and revealed the complete awareness which abides in unborn state of nirvana. I knew I had gained great wisdom, and all scriptural doctrines became clear to me.

How was this so?

1. The birth place of the Buddha, the treasury stairway where the Buddha descended from the Trayastrimsas Heaven, the place where the Buddha attained Enlightenment, and the places where the Buddha turned the Dharma Wheel, are places where there are gatherings of countless buddhas and bodhisattvas, as well as the eight divisions of spiritual beings. These places hold infinite states of samadhi.
2. When we circumambulated the stupa in a clockwise manner, we gained the Six Perfections.
3. By chanting OM, the Dharma Realms of the ten directions are purified.

With an auspicious combination of good timing, positive environmental circumstances, and good human support, to quote from the tantras: "One shall gain great wisdom, rise above all defilements and decide to attain Supreme Perfect Enlightenment."

85. The Mirror Shrine Psychic Hearing Method

To my knowledge, there are many cultivation methods for developing the listening faculty of gathering information by listening to spiritual beings. The Taoist ways include the Spiritual Child Psychic Hearing Method, the Youth of Good and Evil Psychic Hearing Method, and the Spiritual Beings Psychic Hearing Method. In Buddhism, there is the supernatural faculty of divine hearing, and so on. Vajrayana Buddhism has its method of psychic hearing. In the Practice of the Dharani of Cundi Bodhisattva, the Mother of Seven Kotis of Buddhas, it mentions the method of psychic hearing through the mirror shrine. The practice is detailed as follows:

The Buddha says: If a person dwells in quiet meditation, and recites the mantra up to two hundred, four hundred or six hundred thousand times, he shall gain accomplishments in all worldly and transcendental practices. If an ordained Buddhist or a lay Buddhist cleanses his mouth with pure water and faces the East, form the Cundi Bodhisattva Mudra in front of a mirror, and recite the mantra one hundred and eight times for forty-nine consecutive days, there shall follow an auspicious occurrence in which Cundi

Bodhisattva shall command two sages to keep the person in good company. And whenever the person has a question, he shall receive answers from the two sages who shall whisper the information into his ears.

Who are these two sages? The sutra does not reveal their names, but I know their identities: they are none other than the two Dragon Kings Nanda and Upananda. Or they can also be two celestial rulers known as Suddha from Suddhavasa, the Pure Heavenly Abodes.

During the early days, I used to cultivate the Youth of Good and Evil Psychic Hearing Method, which I subsequently taught to my mother. Thus at my home, Ling Xian Jing She [Spiritual Immortal Place] in Taichung, Taiwan were enshrined two statues of the Youth of Good and Evil. One of his hands points to heaven and the other hand points to the earth.

I personally feel that the Taoist art of the Spiritual Child Psychic Hearing Method is of a lower spiritual level, similar to the psychic art of keeping minor ghosts. Those who take the path of proper cultivation should avoid this art. It would be better to learn the Mirror Shrine Psychic Hearing Method. This method utilizes a clean mirror which has not been used previously, and which is set before a statue or painting of Cundi Bodhisattva. Make offerings of flowers, incense, lights, tea and fruits to Cundi Bodhisattva on the night of the fifteenth day of each [lunar] month.

Recite the Cundi Bodhisattva Mantra in front of the mirror, forming the mudra while reciting, and use the mirror as your shrine. In this way, you shall achieve attainment.

Upon the completion of mantra recitation, the mirror must be stored away in a container, as this mirror shrine should not be visible to others. If it were to be seen, accomplishment would be impossible. Therefore, the cultivation of this practice should be kept secret, and should not be disclosed to anyone.

The Mirror Shrine Psychic Hearing Method involves a set of pith instructions which are required for cultivation success. One must request this transmission from the Root Guru.

I once said that in order to achieve results with Vajrayana practices, the personal deity must descend to radiate light. As long as you become one with your personal deity, you shall have success with all dharma practices.

Sheng-yen Lu

86. The Heart of Heart Mudra

When I was learning the Vajrayana teachings, I received the transmission of the special practice of the Heart of Heart Mudra from my guru. My guru told me, "This method should only be imparted in secrecy, so the knowledge remains hidden from others."

"Who can receive this teaching?"

"A heart son!"

What my guru meant was that in Vajrayana Buddhism, there exist many practices which are only transmitted to the right candidate with high spiritual capacity, and also many practices that are only imparted to those with strong spiritual conviction. The Heart of Heart Mudra is among these.

My guru explained that a heart son refers to a disciple whose heart mirrors the heart of his guru, who would not leave and betray his teacher. For example, Marpa looked upon Milarepa as his heart son, and thus passed the lineage to him.

A heart son is hard to come by these days, as people of modern times tend to display a tricky mind which is anything but innocent. With some measure of accomplishment, the individual will claim his superiority over his own teacher. And modern people tend to show little gratitude, as most gravitate towards selfish ends. The trustworthy ones are few, and those who keep a strong and firm spiritual conviction all the way are only a handful.

Therefore, my guru said that the Heart of Heart Mudra must be transmitted to a specially chosen disciple who must be observed for many years prior to this transmission. If the transmission of the Heart of Heart Mudra is given to the wrong person, the guru himself and his lineage would be subjected to great harm, in which the guru might have to take part of the responsibility and be punished by the heavens.

I would not dare reveal the details of the Heart of Heart Mudra here. All I can say is that anyone who learns this teaching would be able to invoke all buddhas, bodhisattvas, arhats, pratyekabuddhas, the beings of the twenty-eight heavenly realms, Indra, Mahabrahma, the Four Heavenly Kings, Lord Yama, the Dragon Kings, the sages, the eight divisions of spiritual beings and other spirits. Once invoked, they arrive immediately.

I once said that in order to achieve results with Vajrayana practices, the personal deity must descend to radiate light. As long as you become one with your personal deity, you shall have success with all dharma practices. You can see how vital it is to master the Heart of Heart Mudra.

Most Vajrayana lineage gurus considered the Heart of Heart Mudra a special teaching, and would only transmit it to the heart son. If it is imparted to the wrong candidate, it would only bring misfortune.

87. Oratory Practices

When I first graduated from my studies, my guru told me, "In the future, you will be spreading the Dharma to the world. But your natural disposition is to be quiet, so you are not someone who is eloquent or articulate. How should we resolve this?"

I was indeed reticent in my ways and fit all the descriptions of an introvert. I had stage fright whenever I needed to give a speech, and in a halting voice I said to my guru, "Master, please teach me a way to resolve this!"

My guru then told me, "First visualize the syllable RAM on the tongue, and then visualize the syllable transforming into the syllable HUM. Following that, recite OM RAM HUM one hundred and eight times, and your tongue shall become more active!"

My guru also transmitted another practice to me: visualize an eight-petalled lotus flower arising from the throat chakra. On the lotus flower is the syllable AH. Visualize the syllable AH transforming into a moon disc, which subsequently changes into the syllable HUM. The syllable HUM then transforms into a five pronged vajra. Visualize this vajra move up to the tongue. This is known as the "vajra tongue." After this visualization, recite the three syllable mantra of OM AH

HUM one hundred and eight times. After doing this, you would become very eloquent in your oratory and debating skills.

Subsequently, I received another practice: the heart chakra of the practitioner transforms into an eight-petalled lotus moon disc. The center of the moon disc is imprinted with the Sanskrit syllable DHI. Above the syllable is lined the heart mantra of Manjushri Bodhisattva, OM AH RA PA CA NA DHI. The heart mantra then transforms into Manjushri Bodhisattva's Sword, and the tip of this sword is aligned with the tip of the practitioner's tongue. The practitioner then moves his tongue up and down and from side to side, and then recites the heart mantra of Manjushri Bodhisattva one hundred and eight times. The practitioner makes a prayer and dedication:

May Manjushri Bodhisattva bless my vajra tongue so that it facilitates the expounding of Dharma
To what end does facing the wall in meditation lead?
It serves to open the heart so that one may see the original source
Upon the Dharma throne sits a son of Buddha
Everything he expounds naturally falls into place

When you attain accomplishment with this practice, you will become a most eloquent and articulate speaker, for your words shall be gems of truth. You shall reach and deliver countless sentient beings in the most convincing way, and attain the highest path together.

88. The Secret to Opening the Heart Chakra

The Vajrayana approach to seeing the Clear Light begins with first observing the drops, following which one sees the vajra chain, then the vajra screen, and lastly the Pure Land of the Buddhas. At this stage, the practitioner is skilled with the divine eye.

To attain the five eyes and the six supernatural abilities, it is of vital importance to first open the heart chakra and radiate light from the heart.

I shall here impart an extremely precious practice for opening the heart chakra.

First, one should cultivate the vital winds, channels and drops, causing the blazing and dripping action to take place at the heart chakra. This means lowering the drops and raising the inner fire so they meet at the heart chakra, where the water and fire merge. In this way, the heart chakra will open.

The Vajrayana practitioner visualizes himself as completely pure, transparent and spotless, like lapis lazuli. Within this inner emptiness a red, rootless eight-petalled lotus is seen at the heart chakra. Upon the lotus sits a moon disc and on the center of the moon disc is the syllable HUM. Along the edge of the moon disc is a clockwise arrangement of the mantra OM GURU LIAN SHENG SIDDHI HUM. Visualize that each syllable spins in a complete circle, and each syllable radiates brilliantly. It is not necessary to visualize the syllables growing, nor should one enlarge the moon disc in your visualization. The smaller the size of syllables and moon disc, the better.

This technique of meditating and visualizing the mantra OM GURU LIAN SHENG SIDDHI HUM is known as the "Eight Syllable Wheel of the Heart Visualization Practice," which can help open the heart chakra.

Upon the completion of visualization, imagine the lotus and moon disc being absorbed into the syllable HUM. This syllable HUM shrinks into a light drop which surges up to the crown chakra, and in an instant dissipates into the vastness of space as countless dots of light. At once, you shall feel "I am space and space is me." There is nothing to be attained, and the reality of Tathagata is as it is.

Let me reveal this spiritual level of attainment. It is exactly the state of enlightenment revealed in the *Heart Sutra* by the line "Avalokitesvara Bodhisattva, when practicing deeply the Prajnaparamita, perceived that all five skandhas in their own being are empty."

Eighty four thousand wonderful forms
May express the appearance but not the original nature of Amitabha Buddha
It may seem far away, across tens of trillions of Buddha lands
The pure land is really within your heart

Very well. Very well.

89. All the Sadhanas of True Buddha School

All the sadhanas of True Buddha School transmitted by Living Buddha Lian-sheng, Sheng-yen Lu are really a simplified version of the sadhanas of all deity practices as outlined in Tibetan Buddhism. A single cultivation session requiring three to four hours to complete is simplified to a process that takes about forty minutes without losing its essence. This is most suitable to the busy pace of people living in modern times.

The cultivation sadhana is divided into three sections.

The preparatory practices include:
Invocation
The Great Homage
Mandala Offering
The Fourfold Refuge
The Four Immeasurables
Armor Protection
Recitation of the *High King Avalokitesvara Sutra*

The main practices include:

Visualization
Forming the Mudra
Mantra Recitation
The Nine Cycle Breathing Exercise
Entering into Samadhi

The concluding practices include:
Verses of Praise
Prayers
Repentance
Dedication

In the sadhanas of Tibetan Buddhism, the invocation begins with invoking the lineage Root Guru to bless the completion of the cultivation. This is to illustrate that one should never forget the Root Guru. Recite the Guru's Heart Mantra seven times, twenty-one times or forty-nine times. Then begin the stages of cultivation. The lineage gurus felt that such a cultivation of progressive stages would yield better results.

I would like to personally emphasize to all True Buddha School disciples: you must focus and take great care to experience the process of visualization, mantra recitation, mudra and the pith instructions in every stage of the sadhana. Put your heart into ensuring the sadhana is practiced to perfection, and in so doing, cultivate diligently day after day without ever losing your initial spiritual motivation. If you can achieve this, you shall certainly attain buddhahood in this lifetime.

Let me say this. If you are traveling by air for an overseas trip, you can go straight to the main practices. If you are unable to do so, just proceed with mantra recitation.

90. The Great Perfection

The Buddha said, "To cultivate by listening and contemplation, one develops discipline, meditative concentration and wisdom. And in so doing, all that one cultivates and attains shall be in accordance with the Ultimate Principle of Reality and experiential wisdom. A bodhisattva, following a good guide, shall always remember the right teachings that he has heard, and through his recollection of the teachings he learns to make observations. By his observations he contemplates according to the fundamental truth, and with this contemplation he is able to maintain pure discipline. By keeping his discipline, he practices the Ten Virtues. Through the cultivation of the Ten Virtues he practices the Three Pure Conducts. With the cultivation of these three conducts, he behaves responsibly, and with responsible behavior, he develops skillful wisdom. With this skillful wisdom, he develops the Six Perfections. With the Six Perfections he shall develop his bodhicitta. And acting in accordance with bodhicitta he shall develop the great compassion of a bodhisattva.

"As well, a good guide can propagate the path, transmit the teachings, resolve problems and kindle the spiritual lives of men. Thus he can be relied upon. He realizes the truth of impermanence, and thus is diligent in his cultivation. He follows the precepts and therefore avoids creating transgressions. He acts according to the scriptural texts and avoids delusion. He sets up the mandala shrine and recites mantras, through which he gains the enhancement of blessing and wisdom. By penetrating deeply into the truth of a teaching, he therefore achieves one-pointedness. He dwells in profound states through meditation, and thus attains the purification of the mind. He acts properly according to the Six Perfections and therefore gains the wisdom to serve others. His bodhicitta and great compassion are expressed spontaneously and as naturally as he wishes, and he can therefore repay the Fourfold Gratitude, attain the Great Perfection and Supreme Perfect Enlightenment."

Padmasambhava, the second Buddha of Uddiyana, said, "All things of this world are but emptiness. And as humans born in this plane of existence, know that it is pure suffering. Impermanence arrives swiftly, and we must cultivate early. Only he who honors the guru, treasures the dharma and practices diligently shall attain enlightenment!"

Many disciples have asked me, "What is the empowerment of the Great Perfection?"

My reply was, "Where is your mind?"

My disciples were unable to understand what I was implying. Therefore, I explained that all of the Buddhadharma is born of causal conditions, yet the self-nature is inherently empty. There is no person who takes action, nor anyone who receives action. Once this is understood, the route to realizing nirvana is within your reach.

"Emptiness of self, emptiness of others, emptiness of all things, and emptiness of both self and all things." This is the empowerment of the Great Perfection. According to Vajrayana Buddhism, the first of the four levels of empowerment is the empowerment of the purification of the body, speech and mind. The second level of empowerment involves the vital winds, channels and drops. The third level of empowerment involves the Highest Yoga Tantra and the fourth level of empowerment is the Great Perfection.

The Great Perfection is without form, unrestricted, and without a pattern. Therefore, it is an empowerment which cannot be described.

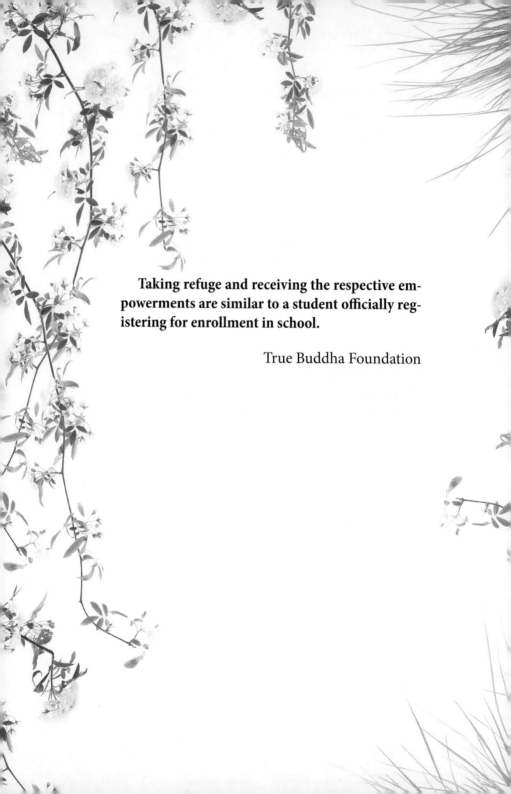

Taking refuge and receiving the respective empowerments are similar to a student officially registering for enrollment in school.

True Buddha Foundation

Significance of Taking Refuge

Taking refuge means to accept guidance, reliance and deliverance.

The heart of taking refuge lies in one word: faith. Faith is the beginning of all endeavors, just as the saying goes:

Faith is the basis of the path, the mother of virtues;
Nourishing and growing all good ways,
Cutting away the net of doubts,
Revealing the unsurpassed road to enlightenment.

The doctrine of faith, understanding, practice, and realization as taught in Buddhism begins with faith.

Taking refuge and receiving the respective empowerments are similar to a student officially registering for enrollment in school. When one receives the empowerment from Living Buddha Lian-sheng and takes refuge in him, one also receives the lineage transmission of True Buddha School and formally becomes a disciple of the school. One's negative karma gradually dissolves, and one is protected by the thirty-six benevolent deities. One also receives all kinds of merits, and does not easily fall into the Three Evil Paths. Therefore, one is able to swiftly accumulate good karma, and eventually realize supreme enlightenment.

From the discussion above, one can thus see that the ritual of taking refuge and empowerment is a holy and noble undertaking. Once one receives the refuge empowerment, one truly enters the gate of practicing Buddhism and becomes a True Buddha disciple.

However, taking refuge is not the same as ordination (becoming a monk or nun). Any ordination must have the written and signed consent from one's parents or spouse, and it must be officially approved by the highest authority of True Buddha School.

The Sutrayana tradition practices the Threefold Refuge, whereas the Vajrayana tradition practices the Fourfold Refuge.

In the Fourfold Refuge, the meaning of the Sanskrit word "Namo" is to take refuge.

> **Namo Guru bei - I take refuge in the Root Guru.**
> **Namo Buddha ye - I take refuge in the Buddha.**
> **Namo Dharma ye - I take refuge in the Dharma.**
> **Namo Sangha ye - I take refuge in the Sangha or the ordained.**

Significance of Taking Refuge in Living Buddha Lian-Sheng and True Buddha School

The Merits of Taking Refuge

Living Buddha Lian-sheng has the dharma title of "Great Blessing Vajra" and he is the Root Guru of True Buddha School. True Buddha disciples who cultivate the Root Guru Practice will be able to achieve spiritual union and responses from the Root Guru, which is a great blessing. With the Root Guru's blessing, one can gain health, long life, a harmonious family, fortune, wisdom, and the fulfillment of all wishes in the mundane realm. In the transcendental realm, one attains bodhisattvahood.

According to the *Sutra of Consecration,* students are protected by thirty-six guardians after taking refuge, which are sent by the Four Heavenly Kings (devarajas). If these students can also cultivate the Root Guru Practice, then Vajrayaksa, his retinue of five hundred, and multitudes of bodhisattvas will also provide protection.

All students who take refuge and receive the necessary empowerments shall, through the diligent cultivation of the Root Guru Practice, benefit both themselves and others due to the boundless merits of the Root Guru Practice. All transgressions will be extinguished and all evil shall depart. The Root Guru Practice is the most efficacious of all practices and should be widely propagated.

The Methods of Taking Refuge

At 7:00 a.m. (your local time), on either the first or the fifteenth of every lunar month, face the direction of the rising sun. With palms joined, reverently recite the Fourfold Refuge Mantra three times: "Namo Guru bei, Namo Buddha ye, Namo Dharma ye, Namo Sangha ye. Seeking Living Buddha Lian-sheng's guidance, I am taking refuge in the True Buddha," and prostrate three times.

Send a letter to the True Buddha Foundation to indicate your wish to receive the refuge empowerment. State your name, address, age, and enclose a voluntary offering to the contact address of Living Buddha Lian-sheng. Upon receiving the letter, the True Buddha Foundation will process your request. The address is:

Grand Master Sheng-yen Lu
17102 NE 40th Ct.
Redmond, WA 98052
U.S.A.
Tel: 425-885-7573
Fax: 425-883-2173

Upon receiving the refuge request letter, the True Buddha Foundation will send you a refuge certificate, a picture of Living Buddha Lian-sheng, and instructions on how to start cultivation of the Four Preliminary Practices.

You may obtain refuge empowerment personally from Grand Master Lu, or from a True Buddha acharya who confers the empowerment on behalf of Grand Master, by visiting a True Buddha temple, chapter, cultivation group, or by attending a True Buddha ceremony.

Glossary

-A-

Amitabha Buddha
One of the Five Dhyani Buddhas, he leads the Lotus Family of buddhas. He is typically depicted with a red body and forming the Meditation Mudra.

Ananda
One of the Buddha's ten great disciples, he was a devout attendant and also a cousin of Shakyamuni Buddha. Among the Buddha's many disciples, Ananda had the most retentive memory and many sutras are attributed to his recollection of the Buddha's teachings during the First Buddhist Council.

Arhat
One who has conquered the emotions and ignorance that keep one locked in samsara, achieved the goal of the Theravada (Hinayana) tradition, experienced the cessation of suffering, and attained the state of liberation.

Asura
One of the six realms within samsara. Beings in this realm are characterized as being very jealous and prone to fighting and arguing with beings in the realm of heaven.

Avalokitesvara Bodhisattva (Chinese - Guanyin, literally "Observes the Sounds of the World")
The bodhisattva of great compassion, with various forms including

the two armed, four armed, or the thousand-armed Avalokitesvara. Guanyin is one of the most important bodhisattvas in Buddhism and is a personal deity in True Buddha School. Guanyin is usually depicted as female in China and Japan, and as male in other parts of Asia.

-B-

Bodhicitta (Sanskrit, literally "Awakened Mind")
The key to Mahayana Buddhism, it refers both to an enlightened mind and to the resolution arising for the profound compassion to attain an enlightened mind for the purpose of assisting all sentient beings.

Bodhisattva
An enlightened being who, out of compassion, forgoes nirvana to help save others.

Bodhisattva Vows
A set of vows taken by those who aspire bodhisattvahood or buddhahood. There are different versions of Bodhisattva Vows.

Brahma
One of the three primary deities of Hinduism - the other two being Vishnu (the preserver) and Shiva (the destroyer). He is usually depicted with four heads, four faces, and four arms.

Brahmanism
The religious beliefs and practices of the Brahmin caste of Hinduism.

Buddhadharma
The teachings of Buddhism.

Buddha-nature
Possessed by all sentient beings, any sentient being may achieve enlightenment by realizing their original nature, which is Buddha-nature.

-C-

Chakra (Sanskrit, literally "Wheel")
Subtle energy centers in the human body, which can be used in internal spiritual cultivation.

Cundi Bodhisattva
Sometimes referred to as the Mother of All Buddhas, she is one of the personal deities of True Buddha School. She is depicted as being light yellow in color, has eighteen arms and a third eye on her forehead.

-D-

Dakini
Dakinis are female wisdom beings who often are protectors of Vajrayana practitioners.

Deva
Gods or heavenly beings. Due to their good merit, they are able to enjoy the pleasures of heaven but are still in the cycle of samsara and will eventually be reborn in another realm.

Dharani
Generally a long mantra. Examples of dharanis include the Great Compassion Dharani and the ironically named Surangama Mantra, which is actually very long.

Dharma
Dharma has two general meanings in Buddhism. The first meaning refers to the Buddha's teachings, while the other refers to any or all things and phenomenon.

Dharma Wheel
An eight-spoked wheel used as a symbol to represent the teachings of Buddhism, the Dharma. "Turning the dharma wheel" means to teach and spread Buddhist teachings.

Dharmakaya (also known as the Truth Body or the Dharma Body) The true nature of the buddha - one that transcends reality, time, form and is one with everything in the universe.

Diamond Sutra
An important teaching of Shakyamuni Buddha which he shows that all things are ultimately empty and devoid of any inherent reality, including the ideas of self, other sentient beings, and the dharma.

Dzogchen
See Great Perfection.

-E-

Eightfold Path
One of the main teachings of the Buddha that shows the way to end suffering and to enlightenment, and makes up the last of the Four Noble Truths. They are: right view, right intention, right speech, right action, right livelihood, right effort, right mindfulness, and right concentration.

Emanation Body (Nirmanakaya)
In order to teach humans, buddhas and bodhisattvas will take a
flesh and body human form (an emanation body) to come and teach
sentient beings. Amitabha Buddha has taken the form of Living
Buddha Lian-sheng to teach the dharma in this present day and age.

Eminent Sanshan-Jiuhou
Living Buddha Lian-sheng's first teacher who manifested out of the
spiritual realm, teaching him many Vajrayana practices.

Empowerment
A ritual wherein the guru transmits to a student the initiation of a
particular deity or practice so that the student is allowed to cultivate
it.

-F-

Fifty Stanzas on Guru Devotion
Written by Master Asvaghosa, this work defines the etiquette
disciples must adopt to show their respect to their guru. Disciples
of Vajrayana Buddhism must follow these rules and show utmost
dedication to their guru if they hope to have accomplishment in
their practices.

Five Herukas
The five herukas of Tibetan Buddhism are: (1) Hevajra; (2)
Chakrasamvara; (3) Mahamaya; (4) Guhyasamaya; (5) Yamantaka.

Five Precepts
The five basic precepts of Buddhism: (1) do not kill; (2) do not steal;
(3) do not commit sexual misconduct; (4) do not lie; and (5) do not
take intoxicants.

Five Wisdoms

The Five Great Wisdoms are: (1) the Wisdom of Ultimate Reality (of Vairocana Buddha); (2) the Great Mirror-like Wisdom (of Akshobhya Buddha); (3) the Wisdom of Equanimity (of Ratnasambhava Buddha); (4) the Wisdom of Discriminatory Awareness (of Amitabha Buddha); (5) the All-accomplishing Wisdom (of Amoghasiddhi Buddha).

Four Noble Truths

The first and fundamental teaching of Shakyamuni Buddha. These truths are: (1) the truth of suffering; (2) the truth of the cause of suffering; (3) the truth of the cessation of suffering; (4) the truth of the path to the cessation of suffering.

Four Preliminary Practices

These practices remove hindrances and build merit so that one may have greater success in cultivation. They consist of: (1) the Great Homage; (2) the Mandala Offering; (3) Fourfold Refuge Mantra; (4) the Vajrasattva Yoga.

Fourfold Refuge

Taking refuge in the Root Guru, the Buddha, the Dharma and the Sangha.

-G-

Ganges

A famous river in India frequently mentioned in Buddhist sutras. The Buddha spent a lot of time near the Ganges and many Indian people at that time could relate to the metaphors in which he used the Ganges, i.e., "the number of sentient beings that would be liberated by the Buddha would be as numerous as the stars that fill the sky, like the sands of the Ganges."

Golden Mother of the Jade Pond
A major Taoist deity, she is associated with the peach of immortality, and she bestows longevity to sentient beings. She helped Living Buddha Lian-sheng begin his spiritual practice and therefore is usually one of the primary deities on True Buddha School temple altars.

Great Compassion Dharani
A long mantra spoken by Avalokitesvara Bodhisattva in the *Great Compassion Dharani Sutra.*

Great Mandala Offering
One of the four preliminary practices of Vajrayana Buddhism; through making offerings to the buddhas, the practitioner generates a heart of generosity - this generous heart is then directed toward sentient beings, thus developing bodhicitta.

Great Perfection (Tibetan: Dzogchen)
The supreme teaching of the Nyingmapa sect; through this accomplishment, one recognizes the purity of the mind that has always been present and realizes the union of emptiness and wisdom.

-H-

Heruka
There are enlightened beings (buddhas) who take on wrathful forms, subdue evil forces, and protect Buddhist practitioners.

High King Avalokitesvara Sutra
The sutra includes the names of many buddhas and bodhisattvas of the ten directions and three times and has been in circulation since China's Tang Dynasty. To chant the *High King Avalokitesvara Sutra* is

equivalent to receiving blessings from the buddhas and bodhisattvas of the ten directions.

Highest Yoga Tantra (Sanskrit: Anuttarayogatantra)
This is an extremely high level of teachings in Tibetan Buddhism. The practitioner utilizes subtle energies and consciousness, which are not accessible to the untrained practitioner, to attain buddhahood.

Homa (Fire Offering)
A fire ritual used as a means of offering to buddhas, bodhisattvas, dharma protectors or other spiritual beings.

Huineng (the Sixth Patriarch of Chinese Zen Buddhism)
A Chinese Zen Patriarch who was one of the most important figures in the entire tradition. He is known for expounding the *Platform Sutra of the Sixth Patriarch*.

-I-

Indra
In Hindu mythology, he is the supreme deity amongst all the deities in the heavens. He governs the thirty-three heavens within the Trayastrimsa Heaven, which is a heavenly realm above the realm of the Four Heavenly Kings, on top of Mount Sumeru.

Inner Fire Yoga (Tibetan: tummo)
Meditation practice commonly associated with the subtle channels, intense sensations of body heat, drops, and vital winds. It is one of the techniques of the Six Yogas of Naropa.

-J-

Jambhala

There are five Jambhalas: (1) the White Jambhala; (2) the Red Jambhala; (3) the Yellow Jambhala; (4) the Green Jambhala; (5) the Black Jambhala. The Yellow Jambhala is a personal deity in True Buddha School. Jambhalas are able to grant abundance and wealth to those cultivating his practice, allowing the individual to practice the Buddhadharma and to help others.

-K-

Kalpa

Refers to the length of time between the beginning of each universe and can be subdivided into twenty smaller kalpas.

Kanjurwa Khutughtu

Kanjurwa Khutughtu was a great tulku (living buddha) and was the head of the Gelug sect in Mongolia. One of Living Buddha Lian-sheng's Kalachakra lineages comes from him.

-L-

Lama

A guru or spiritual teacher in Tibetan Buddhism, who is seen as the embodiment of a buddha.

Lord Yama (Lord of Death)

He is known as the king of the netherworld and the head of karmic punishment of those who reside in hell.

-M-

Maha Twin Lotus Ponds
This is the pure land of Padmakumara located in the Western
Paradise of Amitabha Buddha. By practicing the True Buddha
Tantra, one may travel to the Maha Twin Lotus Ponds in meditation
or at the time of death.

Mahamudra (Sanskrit, literally "Great Seal")
The central teaching of the Kagyu sect of Tibetan Buddhism.

Mahayana Buddhism (Sanskrit, literally "Great Vehicle")
The branch of Buddhism which emphasizes liberating all other
sentient beings from suffering before attaining enlightenment. It
became the dominant form of Buddhism in East Asia.

Maitreya
The future buddha of this aeon, Maitreya Bodhisattva, is presently
residing in the Tushita Heaven.

Mandala
It is a symbol which represents the realms of buddhas, bodhisattvas,
or dharma protectors. It may be in two dimensions, as in a painting,
or in three dimensions, such as in the placement of sacred objects.
The representations are very artistic with intricate colors and designs
to aid in visualization.

Manjushri Bodhisattva
He is the bodhisattva of Transcendent Wisdom. He is typically
depicted with a lotus holding the *Prajnaparamita Sutra* and a sword
of wisdom which cuts through ignorance.

Mara
Demons or demonic influences which are analogous to as what is

commonly known as "devil" in Christianity. They can manifest in many forms, such as the forms of greed, anger, ignorance, jealousy, and other emotions.

Marpa
A great forefather of the Kagyu lineage of Tibetan Buddhism. Regarded as an emanation of Hevajra, he was also known as Marpa Lotsawa, or Marpa the Translator. He travelled from Tibet to India three times to bring back various Vajrayana Buddhist teachings which he translated, especially those of his guru, Naropa. He also studied under Maitripa.

Master
See Vajra Master.

Milarepa
Another forefather of the Kagyu lineage. He was a student of Marpa and practiced in the mountains of Tibet for many years, attaining complete enlightenment. One of his main disciples was Gampopa, who founded the Kagyu School.

Mount Sumeru (also called Mount Meru)
This is the name for a mountain mentioned in Buddhist cosmology. It is surrounded by four continents, with Trayastrimsas Heaven at its top.

Mudra
A mudra is a symbolic or ritual gesture in Hinduism, Buddhism as well as Taoism. While some mudras involve the entire body, most involve using the hands and fingers. In yoga, mudras are used in conjunction with breathing exercises to stimulate different parts of the body involved with breathing and to affect the flow of qi or vital

winds in the body.

-N-

Naga
Nagas are serpent-like spiritual beings living in caves, rivers and heavens who often guard great treasure.

Nagarjuna
Nagarjuna is one of the most important figures in Buddhism. He received the Vajrayana teachings from Vajrasattva, and was able to enter the dragon palace under the ocean and study all the Mahayana scriptures that were being kept there. He wrote the *Madhyamika Sastra* among other important Madhyamika works.

Naropa
A scholar at the famous Nalanda University who left to follow the noted yogi, Tilopa. He is known for the Six Yogas of Naropa which form a major part of the practices of the Kagyu School of Tibetan Buddhism. He was the master of Marpa.

Nirvana
Cessation of suffering where one is freed from the cycle of rebirth. It is a state where one realizes one's connection with the absolute.

-P-

Padmakumara (Sanskrit, literally "Lotus Youth")
The sambhogakaya (bliss body) form of Living Buddha Lian-sheng, a great fortune-bestowing and hindrance removing bodhisattva.

Padmasambhava (Sanskrit, literally "Lotus Born")
Commonly known as the "Second Buddha" in the Himalayas, he was
invited by the Tibetan king Trisong Detsen to establish Buddhism in
Tibet in the eighth century. He established the Nyingma tradition of
Tibetan Buddhism and is one of the personal deities of True Buddha
School.

Pratyekabuddha (Solitary Realizer)
A practitioner who attains nirvana without a teacher, but does not go
on to teach others the path towards enlightenment.

Pure Land
A pure abode founded by a buddha. By being reborn in a pure
land, the aspirant can continue spiritual development towards
enlightenment without fear of falling back into the six realms of
reincarnation.

Pure Land School
One of the schools of Mahayana Buddhism in which the objective
is to be reborn in Amitabha Buddha's Western Paradise. The main
practice of the Pure Land School is to chant the name of Amitabha
Buddha with total concentration, known as recitation of the Buddha
name and mindfulness of the Buddha ("nian fo" in Chinese,
"nembutsu" in Japanese).

-R-

Rainbow Villa
This is the retreat center that Living Buddha Lian-sheng built in the
Cascade Mountains in the western region of Washington State. As
of 2008 it was declared a temple and is now called the "Rainbow
Temple."

-S-

Sadhana
Procedures and liturgy for Vajrayana practices. In general, sadhanas consist of chanting mantras, forming mudras, and visualizations associated with a particular deity.

Samadhi
Deep meditation where the mind becomes serene and there are no thoughts.

Samaya
Samaya means pledge or commitment and is the foundation of Vajrayana training. The samaya includes various commitments and pledges, with the bond between the guru and the disciple being of utmost importance. Examples of samaya pledges include viewing the guru or vajra master as a buddha, and viewing his or her body, speech, and mind as pure.

Samsara
Comprised of the six realms: devas (gods), asuras, humans, animals, hungry ghosts, and beings in hell. Sentient beings are stuck in the six realms until they attain enlightenment, thus freeing them of the need to be reborn in one of these realms.

Sangha
A Sanskrit word meaning "community," "assembly," or "association with a common goal." In Buddhism, it refers to monks or nuns with a higher realization, though in modern times this term has been used to describe groups of Buddhist followers in general.

Sanskrit
The language of ancient India. Sanskrit was the language of the
Hindu Priest Class and the Veda Scriptures. It was later adopted by
Buddhists to record Buddhist scriptures.

Sariputra
One of the Buddha's ten great disciples, he was renowned for his
great wisdom. Sariputra and Maudgalyayana were the Buddha's two
chief disciples.

Sarnath
A place in India where Shakyamuni Buddha gave his first discourse
and introduced the Four Noble Truths.

Sastra
A Sanskrit term that, in a Buddhist context, refers to treatises written
to explain Buddhist sutras or concepts.

Sentient beings
Broadly speaking, all living beings with awareness who have not
attained enlightenment and become buddhas. More narrowly, all
living beings with awareness within the six realms of reincarnation.

Shakyamuni Buddha
Prince Siddhartha Gautama was born in Lumbini sometime between
563 BCE and 483 BCE. He later became known as Shakyamuni
Buddha. "Shakya" was his clan name and "muni" means great sage,
thus Shakyamuni means "the great sage of the Shakya clan." At the
age of twenty-nine he left his home, and achieved enlightenment
under the Bodhi Tree at age thirty-five. He became the founder of
Buddhism and spread the dharma.

Siddhi (Sanskrit, literally "Accomplishment" or "Ability")
Refers to the accomplishments that come with spiritual practice. It may be the transcendental siddhi of attaining nirvana or it may refer to more mundane abilities like the divine eye, clairaudience, etc.

Six Realms
See *Samsara.*

Skandhas
There are five skandhas (or five aggregates) which are: (1) form; (2) sensation; (3) perception; (4) volition; (5) consciousness. Our physical world is the form, and we experience the sensations of sight, sound, smell, taste and touch. Our mind creates distinctions between what it likes and does not like. Based on these likes and dislikes, perceptions are produced which lead to our volition or actions. All of these forms, perceptions of forms, thoughts and actions are stored in our consciousness.

Stupa (Chinese: pagoda; Tibetan: chorten)
Emanating blessings and peace, stupas are venerated Buddhist monuments or shrines frequently containing the relics and sometimes the entire body of an enlightened being or other sacred objects.

Sutra
The teachings of the Buddha which make up part of the Buddhist Canon, the Tripitaka.

Sutrayana
This refers to Buddhist teachings and schools that are based on the sutras that are open for all to read. Also called "Exoteric" Buddhism.

-T-

Talisman
Metaphysical objects infused with the power of the person who draws them. They are drawn onto paper and then burned and eaten, or carried by the person wishing to use the talisman's power. They may be used to help cure illnesses, to protect one from danger, create harmony, etc.

Tantra
Refers to the teachings of Vajrayana. It is the spiritual truth which seeks to unite the individual consciousness with the universal consciousness through various mystical means.

Taoism (Daoism)
The Chinese philosophy in which practitioners seek to realize and be one with the Tao, the primordial source for all things. The yin-yang symbol is a popular symbol of Taoism showing that within the ever changing nature of all things, the Tao is always present.

Tathagata
Sanskrit word meaning one who has thus come. It is one of the titles for buddhas.

Ten Virtues
The Ten Virtues are: (1) no killing; (2) no stealing; (3) no sexual misconduct; (4) no lying; (5) no slanderous or alienating language; (6) no profane or abusive language; (7) no bawdy or lewd language; (8) no greed; (9) no anger; (10) no ignorance.

Three Jewels
The three treasures of Buddhism to take refuge in: the Buddha, the

Dharma, and the Sangha.

Thus Come One
See *Tathagata*.

Trayastrimsas Heaven
A heavenly realm above the realm of the Four Heavenly Kings, on the top of Mount Sumeru. According to tradition the Buddha spent time there teaching the Abhidharma to his mother, who was reincarnated into this realm. There are thirty-three heavens within this realm and all are governed by Indra.

True Buddha Tantra
Created by Living Buddha Lian-sheng based on his experience in practicing all the various systems of Buddhist Tantras. He condensed and simplified the sadhanas and procedures of Tantra cultivation to make it more suitable for people facing the demands of modern society. The core of the progression is aimed at achieving enlightenment. It also includes many ancillary practices for worldly benefits to improve the cultivator's living conditions, thus allowing the cultivator to overcome mundane obstacles.

Truth Body
See *Dharmakaya*.

Tsongkhapa
Founder of the Gelug sect of Tibetan Buddhism who set up strict monastic rules. He is regarded as an emanation of Manjushri Bodhisattva.

Twelve Links of Dependent Origination
These are: (1) ignorance; (2) karma; (3) consciousness; (4) name

and form; (5) the six senses; (6) contact; (7) sensation; (8) desire; (9) attachment; (10) existence; (11) rebirth; (12) old age and death.

-V-

Vairocana Buddha
Also known as the Great Sun Buddha, and called Dainichi Nyorai in Japan. He is one of the Five Dhyani Buddhas and is the central buddha in Shingon Buddhism.

Vajra (also called vajra scepter)
A common ritual object in Vajrayana Buddhist practices which represents a thunderbolt, or diamond, which in turn symbolizes indestructibility. It can symbolize the male aspect of enlightenment (skillful means), whereas the vajra bell represents the feminine aspect of enlightenment (wisdom).

Vajra Guru
See *Vajra Master*.

Vajra Hell
The lowest realm of all hells which one may enter by breaking the Samaya Pledge.

Vajra Hook Mudra
A mudra used to invoke buddhas, bodhisattvas and dharma protectors.

Vajra Master
A supreme teacher within Vajrayana Buddhism (equivalent to the Tibetan term "lama"). The master may conduct ceremonies or bestow teachings and empowerments according to the master's level

of accomplishment.

Vajra Master Thubten Dargye
Vajra Master Thubten Dargye is the Gelug guru of Living Buddha Lian-sheng, and gave him the Highest Yoga Tantra empowerment, among many other empowerments.

Vajrasattva
Major deity of Vajrayana Buddhism. By chanting the Hundred Syllable Mantra of Vajrasattva, negative karma is quickly removed.

Vajrasattva Practice
Major part of the Four Preliminary Practices. It is a repentance yoga to remove karmic hindrances created by past negative actions and by breaking vows.

Vajrayana
A major branch of Buddhism in which the guru teaches an accelerated path to enlightenment, using the techniques of chanting mantras, forming mudras and visualization.

Vase Breathing
This breathing technique uses qi or vital winds to open the channels and meridians in the body.

Vinaya
One of the three parts of the Tripitaka which emphasizes precepts, discipline, vows, conduct and ethics.

-W-

Western Pure Land (Western Paradise, Sukhavati)
The Pure Land of Amitabha Buddha. Many Buddhists aspire to
be reborn there so they may cultivate diligently until reaching
enlightenment, without fear of falling back into the six realms of
reincarnation.

-Y-

Yidam (Personal Deity)
One of the Three Roots (Guru, Yidam and Dharma Protector)
of Vajrayana Buddhism. Practice of the Yidam Yoga begins after
attaining spiritual resonance in the Four Preliminary Practices, the
Guru Yoga and receiving the proper empowerment. A practitioner
should choose a personal deity with whom he or she has the most
affinity with.

Yoga (Sanskrit, literally "Union")
In Vajrayana Buddhism, it is a method uniting an individual with the
buddha, which helps the practitioner reach enlightenment. In this
sense, it is not the same as the yoga practiced worldwide to improve
physical fitness and health.

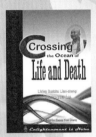